Real Scandinavians
NEVER ASK DIRECTIONS

Scandinavian America, Wit & Wisdom

by
ART LEE

Author of the **Lutefisk Ghetto**,
Leftover Lutefisk and **Leftover Lefse**

Book and cover design by Jonathan Norberg
Published by Adventure Publications
P.O. Box 269
Cambridge, MN 55008
1-800-678-7006

Third Printing
ISBN 1-885061-78-1

PREFACE

Famous radio and TV commentator, the late Eric Sevareid, had it right when he noted: "Childhood in small towns is different from childhood in the city. Everything is home."

Sevareid knew what he was talking about, having been born and raised in a small North Dakota community. Small towns in the upper Midwest had and have much in common, even geographically. That is they simply "stop" where and when the fields and forests surrounding them begin. You're in town; then a block later you're out in the countryside again.

Which rural communities might be labeled "big" in size is often measured by their number of stop lights, with any locality having two stop lights or more regarded, at least by the locals, as a pretty big town indeed. A "big town" is of course a relative judgment, and like the concept of beauty, "bigness" is in the molded eye of the beholder. (Even cities like Minneapolis can be huge; except to Londoners, it's small.)

Another commonality. The hundreds of Midwest Scandinavian ethnic communities once operating in the middle of the 20th century were virtually all "three-generation towns," meaning that living there were the families of grandparents, parents, and children. Before 1950 it was not uncommon that the three generations lived together in the same house, or often the grandparents lived in a small house not far from the main house. (Aging grandparents then were not shuffled off to be institutionalized in some distant nursing home.) Because grandma and grandpa were more than likely emigrants themselves, or at least the children of emigrants, tracing one's ancestry beyond grandparents required going back to the old country. This degree of traveling was seldom done then; nor was genealogy big in 1950. All this has changed, of course, dramatically.

Real Scandinavians has two major sections, the first one—"Then"—deals with the "old" Scandinavians mainly before 1950 while the latter "Now" section concerns the later second, third and fourth generation families—these latter years when both trips to the Scandinavian countries and genealogy have become BIG.

The two final chapters give an assessment on what has happened and what is happening to Scandinavian-American culture as we move into the new century. In many ways this book fits into the current Great Ethnic Reawakening of Americans; it is the author's hope that readers will both enjoy the stories and at the same time learn some things, painlessly.

—*Art Lee*

CONTENTS

IT ALL DEPENDS ON...

A Representative Story, As Told In Sweden

Two retired Norwegian farmers met every Saturday for coffee at the local cafe, and this one morning meeting was preceded by a big snowstorm the night before. When Lars Trulson walked in late, shaking the fresh snow off his pants and sorrel boots, Truls Larson was already sitting there slurping his coffee.

Truls looked up and said to Lars, "Boy! Dat wuss one big snowstorm we had last night, then, and I'm sorry to hear about your wife."

"Ya," said Lars. "I had a tough time gettin' outta my driveway dis mornin' but she went fast. Let's go fishin'."

ONE'S PERSPECTIVE

A Representative Story, As Told In Norway

An American tourist arrived in Norway and took a bus from the airport to Gjøvik, where a friend was to drive down from Lillehammer to meet him. When the waiting friend saw the bus drive up and stop, he got out of his car and only then noticed that nearby a dog was attacking a small child. The man ran to the child's aid. The dog was so fierce in its attack that the man had to throttle the dog to stop the assault.

An hour later there was a knock on the hotel door and standing there was a reporter for the Gjøvik newspaper who had heard about the incident and wanted to write it up in the local paper, complete with picture, on page 1. Said the reporter, "It will read, 'Lillehammer Men Save Children From Pack of Wild Dogs'."

The American said, "But there was only one man, one child and one dog."

"All right," said the Norwegian reporter. "We'll put the story on page 2 with the headline, 'Lillehammer Man Saves Child From Savage Dog'."

The American then said, "But my friend is not from Lillehammer. He's from Sweden."

Upon hearing that, the reporter closed his notebook and walked out the door. When the paper came out that week, there on the last page was a small article with the headline, "Visiting Swede Kills Family Pet."

Scandinavian-America...THEN

- Nostalgia is memory with the pain removed.

- Back in the olden/golden (?) days of grade school, they had sex education, too, except then they called it "recess."

- Truls Larson said he had air conditioning in his 1940 Ford V-8; he called it "40 and 4". He drove 40 miles per hour with all 4 windows rolled down.

Scandinavian Philosophical Conundrum:

There's the familiar riddle about a tree falling in a forest and if no one is there as a witness, will the falling tree still make a noise?

Now the Scandinavian puzzler: If a husband is alone in the forest and talking, and no one is there to hear him, does that mean he is still wrong?

Three things there are for real: God, human folly and laughter. The first two are beyond understanding, therefore let us do what we can with the latter.

MOST IMPROPER TO DISRUPT A LUTHERAN CHURCH SERVICE

Everything seemed proper. Everybody seemed proper. Even most of the cars in the church parking lot seemed proper. The autos were almost all Fords and Chevrolets, except for the car owned by Einar Anderson, that big showoff, who drove a '55 Buick. Not only was it different, and fancy, it was two-toned, making it really stand out from the others, which was, of course, a breach of properness.

One farmer, who lived out on the Hesseldal place, being cognizant of local values, had once bought a brand new car, but stored it in his machine shed for a year before daring to drive it to town. On his first trip to Main Street, he replied to the expected nosy inquirers that, "Ya, it's a year-old used car, den." That made it proper.

In their small community, where everyone knew everyone, stood their small Lutheran church, where everyone not only knew everyone, but knew everyone's car, too. That's why there was some head scratching that Sunday morning as parishioners walked by a brand new Studebaker on their way to the side entrance of the building. There, of course, a front entryway but only strangers used it, and that morning, when head usher Oskar Gunderson saw someone come through the front way, he noted that the man went and sat by Rufer and Gladyce Medal, so likely he was with them, Oskar guessed.

The Reverend Nils Swenson looked proper. With his large size, his white hair, his black eyebrows, his advancing years and the voice of a hog caller, he seemed like an Old Testament prophet, or at least what a prophet is supposed to be like.

The holiest hour of the week arrived. Exactly at 11 a.m. Oskar was there in the balcony to pull on the rope that would ring the belfry bell exactly 12 times, one proper pull for each apostle. This was the signal for organist Belva Tostenrud to start pumping the organ and begin to play the entrance hymn, "Holy Holy Holy," which was the signal for the dozen members of the black-robed choir to meander down the middle aisle and into the choir loft in front. They were supposed to march, but the manner in which they came forward was so varied and staggered and haphazard that it seldom resembled marching. Still, it was proper. The exception here was choir member Alvina Kjendalen, who walked alone up the side aisle and joined the group in the loft. Her action was based on her announced opinion that she could not march but only walk. Such goofy logic was viewed by the congregation as an opportunity for Alvina to be seen by everyone. Not proper.

> In their small community...stood their small Lutheran church, where everyone not only knew everyone, but knew everyone's car, too.

The services continued with the order of worship listed in the front of the black hymnal. The liturgical order was followed carefully, including, when they got to the line in the confessional, the non-listed but expected rising of the voice of Pastor Swenson that read, "We are by nature sinful and unclean." That was the favorite theme of his sermons.

11

When it came time for the Bible readings, Johannes Boe lumbered forth from his pew to a lectern up front and began reading, sort of, from the Old Testament lesson. He was not able to correctly pronounce the Biblical names and the names of the ancient cities he massacred royally, but that was all right. At least he was there. Just allowing laymen to read the morning lessons was viewed as theological revisionism and clearly a giant step toward modernity, although strong opposition continued. ("Dat's sumpin' only a reverend should do, den," said Thorlief Brekke.)

On this reading issue, it took Reverend Swenson a couple of years of fruitless persuasion before he could get any man to come forward to read. At that rate it would take a couple of more years before careful consideration would ever be given to allowing any woman to read. When he was new to the congregation, the pastor had learned their Seven Last Words: "We've never done it that way before."

Actually, Clifford Bredesen loved to read up front, but he'd sometimes get emotional and lose his place and his voice and start to blubber, and that was no good. Not proper. And schoolteacher Erling Wolden loved to get up front, but before he'd read he'd always give an explanation first and if there's anything they didn't want, it was some didactic message from anyone other than the pastor. Why are schoolteachers forever trying to teach everybody everywhere?

Following the reading, or misreading, came another hymn (why do they pitch them so high?), and an announcement of a church supper (the rich Ladies Aid was planning to make even more money on another Torsk Supper). Then the choir anthem was rendered (Wilhelm Kvistgaard thought it sounded more like pig-rendering), which anthem followed exactly the dictum of the director, Gudren Stopelstad: "Start on pitch and end on pitch, and anything in-between that comes close will be appreciated."

Then it was time for the sermon. Pastor Swenson mounted the high pulpit, a vantage point that allowed him to see all and tell all, even if those viewed preferred not being seen or told anything. He began by reading from the New Testament, from a message from Paul to the Galations, pronouncing the apostle's name in proper Norwegian style, "Pohl." Then the words "so ends the reading" gave the signal for the up-and-down congregation to sit again, but this time to settle in for the lengthy message to follow, which they both expected and wanted–although not too long, please. Or as A.O. Lien was wont to tell anyone who would listen, "Nobody can be saved after 20 minutes." With time in mind, all the men sneaked peeks at their watches as the pastor swung into action.

> The pastor pronounced in apocryphal and stentorian voice, "Christ died for your sins and the sins of all," at which point a voice hollered "AMEN!"

After five minutes, his swinging seemed to shift into droning and the congregation had shifted from listening to half hearing, some to total daydreaming, and a few to slumber. To the anti-Swenson faction–"The Church Killers" –their man had majored in Platitudes at the St. Paul Seminary. And he was halfway through his torpid litany when it happened. The pastor pronounced in apocryphal and stentorian voice, "Christ died for your sins and the sins of all," at which point a voice hollered, "AMEN!"

A bolt of lightning striking the steeple and a scorching ball of fire hurtling down the new blue carpet of the middle aisle could not have shocked that congregation more! Everybody bolted upward. It woke Karl Moen from a deep sleep, wondering frantically where he was, gasping for air and reaching for his heart pills.

Every head turned to stare at the vocal source that was, of course, the stranger with the Studebaker. He obviously was caught up in the sermon and was responding to it the way he would have in his own Baptist church down south, and at that moment the stranger was oblivious to the looks of the startled Lutherans.

Even Reverend Swenson stopped short at the outburst and appeared confused as to what to say next, but he continued, "Christ is the Son of God, the Word of God, the Lamb of God," to which words the stranger yelled, "HALLELUJAH!" Near him sat Roy Notolfson, squirming and fidgeting and sweating and choking his mangled bulletin, hoped for immediate divine intervention in the form of the ground 'neath the stranger opening up and swallowing this crazy man, hoping he would fall in, not deep enough down to be hurt, just far enough down for him to shut up.

Along with the shock, added Lutheran guilt fell on the multitude as they tried to assess the situation calmly. After all, they were sure the stranger was not trying to be obtrusive, nor offensive, nor demeaning, and on that knowledge really hung the guilt. So the man was vocal, a jump-out-of-your-seat kind of apostolic who wished to publicly proclaim his faith, a follower so caught up in the message of the church that he had to share his enthusiasm of being a Christian. In short, the stranger was everything that they were not. They knew that much about themselves. At an evangelistic rally, they could not manage to raise their hands waist high. "Change" meant wearing your brown suit instead of your blue suit to church. Being labeled "the frozen chosen" was a badge of honor, of civility, of Scandinavian culture and heritage. Proper.

What followed was the shortest sermon Pastor Swenson ever delivered. What followed was what the congregation believed was the longest sermon ever delivered. The stranger's shouts produced mental discombobulation, embarrassment, agony and exhaustion, from white-knuckled anticipation waiting for the next unwanted outburst. When would it come next? And would it be, "AMEN!" or "AMEN, BROTHER!" or "HALLELUJAH!" Some wondered if this nerve-jangling event was the Lutheran version of being held in bondage.

Blessedly, as it were, the service finally ended. Now was the time for hypocrisy. The stranger was greeted warmly with mock enthusiasm and handshakes, welcomed to their church and told to be sure to stop again when he came through. He was told how he really livened up the service–yessir he did–and, "We're not too used to that kind of response, heh-heh," and, "Won't you come downstairs for coffee?" (Thank Gawd he didn't!) And when the interloper drove off in his Studebaker, palpable sighs of relief filled the basement, and the coffee and donuts were devoured in an atmosphere of wonderful deliverance.

Finally, everything was PROPER again.

YOU KNOW YOU'RE A
Lutheran WHEN...

✔ You can identify with all the characters in Lake Wobegon.

✔ You carry silverware in your pocket to church just in case there's a potluck.

✔ You have an uncontrollable urge to sit in the back of any room.

✔ You think lime Jell-O with cottage cheese and pineapple is a gourmet salad.

✔ You think that an ELCA Lutheran bride and an LCMS groom make for a "mixed marriage."

✔ Hills Bros. has you on its Christmas list.

✔ Missouri Synod Lutherans refer to St. Louis as "the holy city."

✔ The only mealtime prayer you know is "Come, Lord Jesus."

✔ You're forty-seven years old and your parents still won't let you date a Catholic.

✔ You know you can't get into heaven without bringing a hot-dish along.

✔ You regard a lottery ticket as a serious investment.

✔ You make your hot dishes with cream of mushroom soup.

☑ You sing "Stand Up, Stand Up For Jesus" while sitting down.

☑ You feel guilty about not feeling guilty.

☑ It's 110 degrees outside and you still have coffee after services.

☑ The most mail you receive all year is from the Stewardship Committee.

☑ You hold your family reunion in the church basement.

☑ Your biggest fundraisers are bake sales, not bingo.

☑ Shaking the hand of a total stranger when forced to "share the peace" can cause trauma.

☑ All the hot dishes at the potluck supper have the owners' names on the bottoms.

☑ All your relatives graduate from a school named Concordia, Luther, St. Olaf, Augustana or Augsburg.

☑ You don't question why the seat you sit in at church is called a "pew."

☑ The new preacher learns the Seven Last Words of your congregation: "We've never done it that way before."

"JUST A FEW PENNIES SHORT..."

An explanation, of sorts: Despite my writing three different books on Scandinavian-America: The Lutefisk Ghetto, Leftover Lutefisk and Leftover Lefse, some hometown readers who were knowledgeable about characters mentioned–or characters not mentioned–reminded me that I had omitted telling even one story about a figure who was among the greatest characters of all, Apple Annie. They're right. Indeed, there is not one older adult in the area today who could not tell at least one Apple Annie tale. This article, then, is to make up for those earlier omissions. Annie deserves some ink.

Her real name was Anna Engell Venedict Smith. However, not one person in a thousand knew her full name as, indeed, knew her by any other name than Apple Annie.

In an odd way she was famous–locally, that is. At least her financial dealings were famous (actually, infamous). Because of her dealings, an "Apple Annie deal" came to be defined as any successful business transaction that by definition fell somewhere between shrewdness and deceit. The latter term was preferred by most.

Annie's nickname came appropriately enough from her having apple trees in her front yard, and year after year she peddled those apples door to door, town to town, with successful sales only to the uninitiated. Those who knew her or had bought apples from her before knew full well that underneath the good layer of apples on top lay rotten apples underneath. By age fifty–and likely long before that–Apple Annie was a con artist, and apples were only part of her operation.

When shopping in stores, Annie used one phrase so often that it became associated with her name, the single phrase, "just a few pennies short." When she purchased items, always in smallest quantities–an eighth of a pound of hamburger, one carrot, a quart of gasoline in a Mason jar–she would inform the clerk at the till at pay-up time that unfortunately she was "just a few pennies short." Those in line mumbled as she searched slowly and methodically through her *penge-pung*, her little black money purse. After this long delay and futile search for funds, she would look up sweetly at the clerk and add, "But I'll bring the rest in tomorrow."

> ...an "Apple Annie deal" came to be defined as any successful business transaction that by definition fell somewhere between shrewdness and deceit.

New or unknowing clerks would usually say at this point to this nice old lady who looked so poor, "Aahhh, sure, then. That's O.K. You bring the rest of the money in tomorrow." But there was no tomorrow. Or when tomorrow came, Annie did not. Score another one for Annie.

Annie was a tallish, slender, skinny woman who lived all alone on a small farm she had inherited from her parents, turn-of-the-twentieth-century settlers, and the run-down place lay a couple of miles west of town. Her bleak farmstead stood out in the colorful countryside because it was so stark. The ramshackle, falling-down buildings were devoid of paint. Stunted apple trees surrounded the dingy frame house. The high grass in the yard never experienced a lawnmower in a lifetime. It looked like a true haunted house, complete with broken and boarded-up windows, and black cats and scrawny dogs crawling out from under the broken porches.

One item was totally missing in the house–a bathtub. Another household item seemed to be in short supply–water. Whatever water there may have been seemed to avoid Annie, whose closeness to cleanliness was miles distant. Because there was no clothesline, the few clothes that were washed were hung out to dry on the limbs of her apple trees.

Her attire matched her home. Around the farm she wore feed sacks or gunnysacks held together by nails. On her feet were four-buckle overshoes held together with binder twine. When she came to town, however, she "dressed up." Then she wore ancient clothes, presumably her mother's, layer upon layer. In cold weather she added to her tall, stooped frame a discolored blackish overcoat, which hung down to her ankles.

To the historically minded, Apple Annie very much resembled the famous Hetty Green, she with the title, Witch of Wall Street. The two looked alike and appeared to dress alike–and act alike, too, as each apparently lived for the purpose of making and then protecting her money.

Hetty Green was a millionaire. Annie was not, of course, but all the townspeople believed she was rich. Indeed, it was an accepted "fact" that Annie was loaded. And that she kept her fortune in gold coins hidden in glass jars buried under the floorboards in her kitchen. For protection, it was said, she had a silver-plated, double-barreled shotgun, the shells filled with buckshot, and her skills with said weapon supposedly rivaled that of Annie Oakley. Such was the conventional wisdom. (As it turned out later, she did not have a hidden fortune in gold, a truth determined by a neighbor who, after she died, sneaked into her house to check those same loose floorboards in the kitchen and found underneath only a few silver coins and pennies that had slipped through the cracks.)

Given Annie's situation, it is understandable that a few sympathetic townspeople (my mother among them) viewed Annie as a pathetic figure more to be pitied than laughed at, and felt that she really belonged in some state home for the bewildered. That kindly view held only until personal business was done with Annie, after which came a quick reassessment with most concluding (my father among them) that Annie knew exactly what she was doing and that she really belonged in some state home called a "jail."

Whichever interpretation, a legion of Apple Annie stories built up, to be retold over the years. Several tales revolved around the alleged edible foods served in her home. This category requires a strong stomach. To illustrate, only at Annie's house did one consider the literal meaning of the term "hot dog," and for her another term seemed appropriate, "hot cat." Somehow the lives of small animals around her barnyard seemed rather brief.

Because the locals knew better than to dine at Annie's quasi dinner table–even at threshing time at her place the helping neighbors found some excuse to be absent at mealtime–it would be only unaware "foreigners" who would experience her culinary preparations and later report their regrets. Among the regrets was not having a stomach pump later.

For example, some out-of-town sawyers came to do some logging for her and at dusk they were invited inside for a home-cooked meal. One woodman later told of spying a fat barn cat sitting on the kitchen table, surrounded by plates of food, and that the cat had nabbed a piece of meat from a bowl of stew and had begun to chew on it. Annie then spied the creature in the middle of swallowing the morsel. She ran and grabbed the cat by the neck, dug her fingers down its throat, came out with the gob of meat, then promptly flipped the meat back into the stew bowl. He added that his appetite subsided after that scene.

A cucumber picker was invited in for cake and coffee on a hot August day. He later related the incident, stating that the cake to be eaten looked like chocolate cake, until he got closer and discovered the dark color was caused by multi-layers of houseflies covering the cake. Even before this revelation, he acknowledged that he should never have stayed for lunch as he had seen Annie walk outside with the coffee pot where she dipped water into the pot from the cow tank by the barn.

Food aside, it was finances that made the dominant theme of most stories. Annie's successes came primarily in more distant communities where she was not known. As a presumed penitent she could–and did–cadge money on street corners, tin cup and all, and scrounge entire meals from restaurants, portraying herself as a forlorn, penniless waif on the edge of starvation in this cruel world, which image she did portray nicely when she went into her Academy-Award-winning routine.

Transportation to area communities presented an early problem, one finally requiring her to buy a car of her own (a '39 Chevy). Until then she managed for some time to finagle rides to her destinations, but getting a free ride home again proved more difficult. The latter required successful ploys, among them: (1) convincing a car salesman that she wanted to buy a used car, but needed to try it out first by having him give her a ride (home) in it; (2) finding a clergyman willing to participate in some social gospel work by delivering an old lady to her domicile, an act to remove possible bad-Samaritan guilt from the man-of-cloth, if not from Annie; (3) convincing cattle dealers to drive her home to look at some critters she was planning to sell, which cattle suddenly went off the market when the car pulled into the yard.

Eventually, one cattleman got so fed up with this charade that he gave Annie one last ride home that she would never forget. He drove his truck like some possessed madman! With the accelerator to the floorboard, he careened wildly up and over and around the winding gravel roads, coming close to tipping at each curve, and finally and skillfully pulling a power "U," halting the hot machine at her front door. A shaken Annie slithered out and soon afterward bought a car of her own, the car for which she would buy a quarter's worth of gasoline at a time. With gas at 20 cents a gallon, it could be done.

All in all, in the heyday of Apple Annie in the 1940s, townspeople perceived her as more of a nuisance than a threat. She was thus tolerated at best, with folks only amused if the newest Apple Annie story could supersede the last shenanigan she pulled off. On occasion she could rise to the challenge, as it were, with an especially slick encounter.

After her passing, however, blood relatives sprang forth. No less than 52 second cousins came forward to claim her alleged fortune.

Like the time Annie weaseled a dollar from a farmer near her place, but getting the buck only on her solemn promise that she would pay him back. She did pay, too, in a way that was her style and won her more fame. The next day she pestered the wife of the farmer who had loaned the dollar in the first place about how tough things were until the exasperated wife gave her a dollar bill just to get rid of her. Annie took the money, went directly to the barn to find the farmer and paid off her debt, as promised. So there!

As Annie advanced in years, failing health forced her to live in a nursing home, and there she died on April 20, 1956, at the age of eighty-two. Until that point there was little hint of relatives. No one wanted to fess up that Apple Annie was kinfolk. After her passing, however, blood relatives sprang forth. No less than 52 second cousins came forward to claim her alleged fortune. But there was no fortune, and what funds she did have had been largely drained off in her last years in the nursing home. Nevertheless, each of the 52 cousins received $360, which altogether came to a sizable chunk of money for that time.

The very mention of Apple Annie's name to old-timers living today produces two automatic responses: first, a smile; then a shaking of the head, the signals indicating correctly that yup, she sure was somethin', all right. Perhaps these days some county social worker would seek her out and provide the special help she seemingly needed, but her contemporaries would tell you that Annie "did not need help from nobody!" She was one tough old gal who made her way through the world just fine, thank you.

Apple Annie is long gone now and hardly mourned. But she is missed! She added local flavor and certainly gave people something to talk about other than the weather. As one octogenarian phrased it, "Well, at least she'll always be remembered." That she will. The older locals can still close their eyes and picture this peculiar specter in her long black coat standing forlornly before the store's cash register, explaining so sweetly and sincerely to the man with the outstretched hand that she was "just a few pennies short."

The Streets of Stavangar
(sung to the melody of "The Streets of Laredo")

AS I WAS OUT WALKING ON THE STREETS OF STAVANGAR
AS I WAS OUT WALKING STAVANGAR ONE DAY

I MET A POOR FELLOW DRESSED UP IN A RAINCOAT
DRESSED UP IN A RAINCOAT LIKE A HIPPY IN MAY

I SEE BY YOUR OUTFIT THAT YOUR'RE A NORWEGIAN
IN A WEIRD OUTFIT THAT MAKES YOU LOOK DUMB.

"YES I AM A NORSKIE AND I FISH FOR LUTEFISK
BUT FISHING FOR LUTEFISK IS NOT VERY DUMB.

THE DUMBHEADS ARE THOSE WHO DO **EAT** ALL THAT LUTEFISK
WHO EAT ALL THAT LUTEFISK SO SMELLY AND BAD

AND WE SHIP OUR LUTEFISK ALL THE WAY TO MINNESOTA
ALL THE WAY TO MINNESOTA SO COLD AND SO DRAB

AND THEY SERVE OUR LUTEFISK AT "NORWEGIAN SUPPERS
AT NORWEGIAN SUPPERS WITH LEFSE AND BRØR
   -And fatigmann and rømegrøt and smør.

AND THAT IS THE STORY SO WHOLE SOME AND TAREW;
AND NOW YOU KNOW WHY NORWAY LOVES ALL OF YOU."

WATER, WATER EVERY-WHERE...BUT HARDLY FIT TO DRINK

Americans associate nineteenth century immigrant pioneer farmers with the major problem of finding decent water for household uses, but in the mid-twentieth century it was still a major problem for some farm folks living in northwest Minnesota. A true story of modern "pioneer" farmers.

"Water is a sacred commodity." –Eleanor Norland

Eleanor Norland, born Eleanor Hunter, was raised on a farm in northern Kittson County, Minnesota, her family's land only three miles from the Canadian border and six miles from the North Dakota border. Their farm was homesteaded by Eleanor's immigrant grandfather, but by the time she came along in the 1920s, farm sizes in that region had increased and were farms talked of not in terms of acres but of sections, with 640 acres to a section. Big scale farming. After all, this was the Red River Valley!

And their land was flat, flat, flat. The fact that they could see the lights of Winnipeg 60 miles away suggested the topography of the earth's surface at that point. The closest town for the Hunters was Orleans, then a thriving community. The population of Orleans today is six.

This upper region of the Red River Valley was first settled by immigrant Swedes and Norwegians, with many more of the former than the latter. Swede Country south of them, too. "A t'ousan' Swedes" lived in the appropriately named town of Karlstad, and even more lived south of Karlstad in the small city that the area's older Scandinavians pronounced "T'eef Riffer Falls."

Although there were pockets of Polish and German residents in Kittson County, it was Swedish that Eleanor mostly heard spoken in the nearby towns, and also it was Swedish she heard spoken at recess in the country school she attended (four grades upstairs, four grades downstairs). However, one of her classmates (there were only three students in her class) taught her, inadvertently, how to swear in Polish. The classmate swore so regularly that when Eleanor got angry at him, the Polish words she used seemed to come to her automatically.

> ...that they could see the lights of Winnipeg 60 miles away suggested the topography of the earth's surface at that point.

Ethnically, the Hunters were primarily Danish, with the mother all Danish and the father half Danish and half English; hence the English name "Hunter." There were two children, Eleanor and younger sister Margaret (Peggy), and theirs was real extended family togetherness as there were ten people in the same farmhouse–the four Hunters, plus the two grandparents, plus Mr. Hunter's bachelor brothers–and together they farmed their flat sections.

Their large house (one bedroom downstairs and three upstairs, with one room big enough to hold three double beds) had no electricity, no indoor toilet, no furnace, and worst of all, no "water." A clarification on the latter point for the Hunter farm home and all the surrounding farmhouses: All the water pumped from below the ground was alkali water. Bad stuff. Phew! Alkali water smelled bad (like sulfur), looked bad (dishpan dirty) and tasted worse (like ashes). Only the dozen Holstein cows of the Hunters could drink it, and the cows drank it from an alkali water pond near the barn. Alkali water was more than a foul nuisance. It virtually drove people away. Historically, many farm families in the upper Midwest left their fertile lands because of alkali water.

The Hunters stayed. Water for their household use came to their farm in several ways. Water to drink and for cooking was hauled in big vats (hauled in by sleigh during winters and by trucks in the summers) from a neighbor who lived far enough to the east (10 miles) to have a "magic" well that produced that precious liquid from the ground called "drinking water."

Other kinds of water on the Hunter place were "man-made." Next to the kitchen wood-burning stove stood a 30-gallon crock. One of the kids' winter jobs was to see that the crock was regularly filled with snow. By morning the melted snow became good soft water that could be used for washing, but it was still too dirty for drinking. When winter ended, precious rainwater off the roof was carefully caught in outside rain barrels and the excess rain was troughed and guttered into a big cistern tank in the basement. And if it didn't rain–and too often it didn't–then blocks of ice from a nearby icehouse were thrust into domestic uses. Water of any kind is extra special when you don't have it.

Under these conditions, a common event like bathing was a luxury that had to be limited. A galvanized tub sitting in the middle of the kitchen floor with 2 inches of water in the bottom found the two sisters arguing weekly about who would be first and who would be second and who would have to use that same bath water.

Washing clothes produced another water consumption problem. On their wood-burning cook stove sat a large copper boiler, filled with water from the cistern. Proctor and Gamble hard soap was cut into little pieces and tossed into the boiler. The "good clothes" went in first, and the items were stirred regularly by what was called a "boiler stick." Regular day-to-day farm clothes were washed in an ancient washing machine powered by a gas engine in the basement, with pulleys from the engine coming up through the floor and attaching to the washing machine in the kitchen above. It worked, sort of.

Cold winter nights presented a special problem for sleeping. Everyone slept upstairs since both the front room and the downstairs bedroom were closed off for the winter. The only heat upstairs came from one stovepipe that ran through the floor of one bedroom and up and out through the roof. Prior to the family going to bed, blankets were wrapped around the downstairs stove (fueled with lignite coal) and stovepipe to warm them up; then came a mad dash upstairs to bed and the quick crawling under a mountain of blankets and quilts. When the bedclothes came against the walls, they froze tightly to the walls by morning. Bringing a glass of drinking water to a bedside table meant that the water was frozen solid by sunup. All ten family members slept two to a bed, the peculiar arrangement motivated by one goal alone–warmth. As Eleanor phrased it, "They paired up for heat."

Alkali water smelled bad (like sulfur), looked bad (dishpan dirty) and tasted worse (like ashes).

All of the above would be difficult enough for two little country girls growing up under difficult, if not primitive, conditions, but added to their situation was the death of their mother when Eleanor was six and Peggy, three. Their mother, Marie Hunter, got tuberculosis and was sent to a T.B. sanitarium at Walker called Ah-Gwah-Ching. Three years later, in 1932, she died there at the age of twenty-eight. Moreover, the girls' grandmother died the next year at home, and so the girls lived, she said, "in a house filled with men." Eleanor also added quickly, "We had a happy, loving home life." (Her father did remarry but that was 13 years later.)

That kind of home life included many extra jobs for the girls. By the time she was twelve, Eleanor had full charge of the house. She was also driving their Model-A Ford at that age, but that's another story. When she and her sister got home each afternoon from country school, their first job was to get the fires going and the cold house warmed up. Then came the needed preparation of a big supper for the hungry men. After the meal came washing dishes and pans and general household cleanup. Then to bed at eight o'clock.

To the question about maintaining any of her Danish heritage in things like cooking, the answer was a strong "no."

"No way. No time to even think about that! We just lived–just existed–day after day . . . day after day."

To the question about hearing foreign languages, she said that those people around there who could and did speak a foreign language were looked down on by the rest and sometimes ridiculed. "In our area, people were embarrassed to talk a foreign language (in the 1930s). Only the old people did it and they mainly did it at home."

Her memories of the farm life for the most part were positive and happy, starting with her fond memory of being taken along as a child to the area old-time dances, usually held in some country schoolhouse. There the desks were shoved aside and the grown-ups and kids together danced the night away. When the little kids got tired, one by one they were laid on the coats that were piled up in the little library room off to the side. The more coats there were, the more sleeping kids there were by midnight.

She recalled with a mixture of pride and amusement that her father purchased the first tractor in the area with rubber tires, and that folks came from miles around to gaze at this peculiar machine. She remembered less fondly the extra work, and the needed morning and evening washings connected with separating cream from the milk via the hand-turned separator located in a small room off their kitchen, and shipping the filled cream cans on the night train to the David Park Creamery in Bemidji.

She shook her head in disgust as she remembered the spring rains that turned the Red River Valley mud into the stickiest gumbo ever to bog down a pair of feet trying to walk from one place to another. "You just couldn't walk! It was awful!"

> **When the bedclothes came against the walls, they froze tightly to the walls by morning.**

Her life changed, and her future, too, when she started high school in 1939 in nearby Lancaster. Unlike the majority of farm students then who found a place to live in town during high school years, Eleanor stayed home on their farm and rode a rattletrap bus to and from school each day. At school she met her future husband, Orielle Norland. They were later married on January 12, 1945. They borrowed a car to go on their winter honeymoon to Winnipeg. It was brutally cold that day and the car was cold and the car brakes froze, but they made it.

Returning, they rented their first house in Lancaster for $10 a month. It had no indoor plumbing nor electricity, but it did have decent water! They were on their way–literally, as her husband got a job with the State Highway Patrol. They moved to Bagley for a short time before moving once more to Bemidji in 1957, and continued to live in the house they bought at that time, a large house on Lake

Boulevard overlooking Lake Bemidji.

For the vast majority of farm families throughout America's history, the greatest and most welcome change to the farms and farm homes was the coming of electricity. For the farm folks in Kittson County, however, there was something even better that arrived, something that ended their "pioneer" days: water, drinking water, coming right to the farms! An expensive major long-range county project, "Northern Kittson Rural Water," starting in 1979, led to the digging of six deep wells throughout the county and then to the laying of miles and miles and miles of pipes, which at last brought drinking water to the most remote dwelling. The "sacred commodity" finally arrived, but not until the 1980s. Good things take a while to achieve.

In reflection, how did Eleanor Hunter Norland assess the "pioneer" life she lived as a young person in the flat, alkali-dominated Red River Valley? Her answer: "I wouldn't ever want it for my kids, but I wouldn't trade it for anything."

Interview at the Norland home on December 23, 1997. Eleanor and her husband had three children, ten grandchildren and one great-granddaughter at that time. Eleanor Norland retired in 1990 after working 29 years at First Federal Savings and Loan in Bemidji. Her husband retired in 1989; at the time he was the Sheriff of Beltrami County. With sadness, however, it must be reported that Eleanor Norland passed away on September 11, 1998. She and her husband had made their annual trip to the Minnesota State Fair and there she suffered a major stroke. Hospitalized, she appeared to be making a good recovery and soon returned to their home where her recovery seemed to be even better. However, there came yet another attack and although she did make it to the hospital, doctors were unable to keep her heart going. She was seventy-three years old.

Eleanor as a child

Eleanor (left) with sister and father

Eleanor with her husband, Orielle (c. 1996)

ℱUN WITH FINLANDERS!!

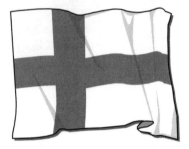

In 100 years, between 1830 and 1930, an "estimated" 2,343,167 immigrants came to America from the five Scandinavian countries: Norway, Sweden, Denmark, Iceland and Finland. To determine the exact numbers from each nation is, of course, impossible, but close approximations are ascribed to all except Finland. Finnish history contributes to this uncertainty in numbers because many Finnish immigrants were listed on the records as Swedes and sometimes Russians. From 1155 to 1809, Finland was dominated by Sweden, from 1809 until 1917, it was dominated by Russia. Modern Finland, as an independent Republic since 1917, is a relatively new nation.

Back to the nose count problem. The "guesstimate" runs that 350,000 Finns came to America; there may have been more/less. Or, as the old joke ran, "Scratch a Swede and you'll find a Finn." Or vice versa. Whatever their exact numbers, the largest settlements of Finns were to be found in Michigan's Upper Peninsula and Minnesota's Iron Range region.

There is much in common among the five Scandinavian countries, with geography being their major connection in Europe. When it comes to languages, however, the one nation having the least in common with the others was/is Finland (Suomi).

Again, like all American immigrants learning English, Finns came out with their own varieties and versions of fractured English. (On a personal note, I had a college friend from the Michigan Upper Peninsula who lived among and worked with Finns, many of whom were immigrants. He loved them; he also loved the way they talked–and he never got over it. On his Christmas card in 1998, he wrote, "As the Finns might say, 'I got the kick out it'.") With that background, and with the likely happening of present-day Finns speaking a perfect King's English, it seems almost useful (historical?) to print (with apologies to those bothered by ethnic stereotyping) the following page:

FINLANDER APPLICATION FOR EMPLOYMENT

Hoos poi you?_____ Vere you livit now?_____

Vat kino blais you livit? Writ pillow:
☐ House ☐ Partment ☐ Hodel ☐ Sauna ☐ Reiler ☐ Ol sack

You kottit tat vamili? ☐ Vife ☐ Pois ☐ Curls ☐ Foks

Vere vas you porn?
☐ Pooskamp ☐ Sauna ☐ Sickenkoop ☐ Soma nudder blais

How you kum tis kuntri? ☐ Pick sip ☐ Lirrol pote ☐ Chet blane

How olt you now?____ Ven you kettit olt aits benson?_____

How you kettit to tis blais?
☐ Puss ☐ Taxi ☐ Railrote ☐ Hits hike ☐ Raivit own kar

Vat kine kar you kottit?
☐ Sevvi ☐ Fort ☐ Woowoo ☐ Tots ☐ Limit

Vat happen you lass chop? ☐ Lait off ☐ Kvit ☐ Ket vired

Vat kine heavi kvipment you oberate?
☐ Booltooser ☐ Reavarmer ☐ Dimerrack
☐ Krate ☐ C.M.C. ruk vit tat hi-pop

Can you oberate tat bower saw?_____

You kottit tat filt poots vit steel toes for vorkit?_____

Vat kine money you vant to keetit here?
☐ Lotsoo ☐ Chust avrits ☐ Jus littoi pit

Vat kina sickness you hat pefore?
☐ Mallbox ☐ Sickenbox ☐ Sookertaipeetus
☐ Boisoning from pat mossine ☐ Pinn-airal tisees (from pirch trees)

You peen tat chale pefore? If so, list pillow howcum

Vat kino ports you like-it?

☐ Kolf ☐ Nooker ☐ Pasket pall ☐ Titlyvinks ☐ Nuddink

If you like-it hunting, vat kine kuns you kottit?

☐ Tree-o-tree ☐ Dirty-dirty vinsester ☐ Too-pipe sotkin ☐ Tveni-too

Vat you like it to hunt for?

☐ Bartrich ☐ Rappits ☐ Teer ☐ Naibors cows ant piks

Vat kine voot you like to eat-it?

☐ Salt fiss ☐ Loot fiss ☐ Sarteens ☐ Melts

Vat you like to rinkitwit?

☐ Puttermilk ☐ Koolait ☐ Peer ☐ Homeproo ☐ Viski

Vat kine moosik you like-it?

☐ Rocket-roll ☐ Pooki-vooki ☐ Noo-vaif ☐ Pookaes

Vat kine nudder lankvits you spik-it?

☐ Rench ☐ Enkliss ☐ Cherman ☐ Nursk

Tank you for answer all tees kvestions.
Memper ven you kum for tat intervoo, you tress-up.
Now you sine tat name on tottet line pillow:

X: --

SURPRISES FOR SCANDINAVIAN IMMIGRANT FARM WOMEN IN AMERICA

Every immigrant to America brought along the same basic "baggage": (1) race, (2) language (plus dialect), (3) culture, (4) religion.

Of the five Scandinavian countries in the late nineteenth century, the nation that was the most rural and whose emigrants became also the most rural, was Norway.

The major waves of emigration from Scandinavia began after the American Civil War ended in 1865. The immigrant arrivals coincided with the new land openings in the upper middle western states and territories (Wisconsin, Minnesota, Iowa, the Dakota territory); hence that region became their primary population center. There were, of course, significant Scandinavian settlements on both coasts, notably in the Brooklyn area of New York City and in Seattle and Tacoma on the West Coast. As to the absence of Scandinavians in the southern states, Scandinavian wags noted later that had their ancestors settled in Georgia or Alabama, they would have been greeting each other with, "Aasen gar det, y'all?" Scandinavian settlement patterns changed somewhat after the turn of the century, with many immigrants locating in Midwestern cities.

However, for the immigrant women who ended up on farms, there were indeed MAJOR SURPRISES:

1. NEVER IN THEIR LIVES HAD THEY BEEN *SO HOT* OR *SO COLD* WITHIN A SIX-MONTH time period.

2. American women wash clothes each week! They do not stand outside to wash and they do not beat the clothes with paddles. They use washboards.

3. American women do not scrub their floors each week!

4. American women do not do field work. (First thing dropped.)

5. American women do not do barn work. (Second thing dropped.)

6. American women do not tend the cattle during the day; kids do that.

7. American women do not wear old-world costumes or clothes. To wear such is the sign of a greenhorn, a foreigner. (Norwegian bunads, colorful, distinctive dress that represented a certain district in Norway, were placed in the back of the closets.)

8. American women do not serve old-world foods except for special occasions and certain holidays, notably around Christmas.

9. American women drink too much coffee, and what coffee they drink is too weak.

10. American women have big families. Each new child is an extra "hired man"; each new baby is a buffer against loneliness.

FOR IMMIGRANT WOMEN THERE WERE INFLUENTIAL WOMEN'S PUBLICATIONS:

1. **Kvinnen Og Hjemmet** (Woman and the Home). Magazine published between 1905 and 1948 (written in Norwegian by a Swede and published by a Dane). Subscription cost: 60 cents a year. High point of circulation: 1912, with 80,000 subscribers. Only mildly feminist; emphasis on "how to Americanize"; one section aimed only at children.

2. **Nylaende** (New Ground). Magazine published between 1887 and 1928. Started in Norway, print ed in America after 1888. Strictly feminist. Emphasized reform and change for women in both jobs and voting rights. Opposed the clear-cut role of women who were expected to get married, stay at home and raise the children; pushed for more women in professions outside of teaching and nursing. (The countries/years when women got THE VOTE: Finland, 1906; Norway, 1913; Sweden, 1919; United States, 1920.)

3. **Decorah Posten**. Weekly newspaper published in Decorah, Iowa, from 1874 to 1972. Nonpolitical. Offered news of Norway and of Norwegian-Americans. Tried to emphasize good literature. Had a section called *Ved Arnen* ("By the Fireside") that serialized entire books. Also featured a cartoon panel (the only Scandinavian publication to do so), Han Ole og Han Per ("He's Ole and He's Per"), the two major goofy characters. Panel drawn and written by Peter Rosendahl, a mainly self-taught artist who was a farmer near Spring Grove, Minnesota, which geographically is close to Decorah. The Norwegian-American Historical Society, Northfield, Minnesota, has published in one volume the complete series of "Ole/Per."

GOD JUL!

BEST EVER RUM CAKE

1 tsp. sugar	1 or 2 quarts of rum
1 cup dried fruit	brown sugar
1 tsp. soda	1 cup butter
2 large eggs	baking powder
lemon juice	nuts

Before starting, sample rum to check quality. Good, isn't it? Now proceed. Select large mixing bowl, measuring cup, etc. Check rum again. It must be just right. To be sure rum is of proper quality, pour one level cup of rum into a glass and drink it as fast as you can. Repeat.

With electric mixer, beat 1 cup of butter in a large fluffy blow. Add 1 seaspoon of thugar and beat again. Meanwhile, make sure rum is till all right. Try another cup. Open second quart if necessary. Add leggs, 2 cups of fried druit and beat till high. If druit gets stuck in beaters, pry loose with drewscriber.

Sample rum again, check for tonscisticity. Next, sift 3 cups pepper or salt (really doesn't matter). Sample rum. Sift in pint lemon juice. Fold in chopped butter and strained nuts. Add 1 bablespoon of brown sugar—or whatever color you can find. Wix mell. Grease oven. Turn cake pan to 350 gredees. Pour mess into boven and ake. Check rum again and bo to ged.

THERE'S NORWEGIAN AND THEN THERE'S... WELL, "NORWEGIAN"

It seems reasonable enough to believe that in Norway the Norwegians talk Norwegian, of course. Not quite. Not only are there two "official" but considerably different forms of Norwegian (see below), but there are over 100 dialects spoken. These regional variations in dialects are so extreme, so different, that Norwegians in some areas can understand almost nothing that those from other areas say!

But back to the two basic "official" forms, one called bokmaal and the other, nynorsk. Attempting to explain each form likely makes it even more confusing for Americans to understand. To illustrate, nynorsk means "new Norwegian" but it is supposed to be really old, old Norwegian that was spoken before the Danes made Norway virtually a colony from 1537 to 1814 and forced Danish bokmaal on the country.

American tourists in Norway who wish to start a hot argument going with any local Norwegians they meet there need only to bring up the language issue and then ask, "Which one is 'correct'?"

Enough for now. Interested readers who are semi-curious about the differences can find them in the two versions of "The Lord's Prayer":

The Lord's Prayer:
Fader vor

Norwegian bokmål

Fader vor, du som er i himmelen!
La ditt navn holdes hellig.
La ditt rike komme.
La din vilje skje påjorden som i himmelen.
Gi oss i dag vort daglige brød.
Forlat oss vor skyld, som vi goforlater vore
  skyldnere.
Led oss ikke inn i fristelse, men frels oss
  fra det onde.
(For riket er ditt, og makten og æren i
  evighet. Amen.)

Norwegian nynorsk

Fader vor, du som er i himmelen!
Lat namnet ditt helgast.
Lat riket ditt koma.
Lat viljen din roda på jorda som i himmelen.
Gjev oss i dag vort daglege brød.
Forlat oss vor skuld, som vi ògoforlet vore
  skuldmenn.
Før oss ikkje ut i freisting, men frels oss fra
  det vonde.
(For riket er ditt, og makta og æra i all æve.
Amen.)

WHEN THE SCHOOL JANITORS WOULD "GO ON A TOOT"

In assessing honestly the supposed "good old days," there was certainly nothing good for those families whose family provider, the husband and father, would "go on a toot." That meant that he would not only get drunk but also stay drunk day and night, with the blurry time period sometimes stretching into weeks. Very strange.

Just the word "toot" is strange. It is not listed in the dictionary with any definition pertaining to prolonged intoxication. (Was it just a Scandinavian-American word? A regional or even a local made-up term? Did other ethnic groups have their imbibers "go on a toot?" Ah, the Great Questions(?) of Western Civilization, or the lack thereof.)

Adding to this peculiar puzzle in my hometown was the propensity for the school janitors to go on such toots, "gone" sometimes for two weeks. Because my father was the supervising principal of the high school at the time, what the thirsty janitors did affected our home life, and in these cases it meant my father was gone a lot doing janitorial work before and after regular school hours. He became quite good at shoveling coal, filling the stokers, and firing up the furnace to get the steam heat going and the bulky radiators clinking and clanking on cold winter days.

The drinking habits of the janitors was such as to add another local phrase, "janitor's vacation." Thus the citizens knew what was meant when someone would in jest indicate that he was planning to set aside a couple of weeks so that he could "pull a janitor."

As a high school student myself at this time (1940s), I could not understand the logic, if indeed there was any, to these extended drinking binges, and questions then brought no answers other than the sniffing put down, "You just don't get it." Now that I'm a retired schoolteacher thinking back on that topic, I still don't get it.

Compounding the riddle of non-explanation of bizarre behavior was janitor Fridtjof Gausen, who went on a toot that ended only with the intervention of the local Lutheran minister, who stepped in after Fridtjof's tenth straight day on the sauce. The results of this pastoral visitation produced one of the strangest solutions to come out of any therapy session. The custodian informed the pastor that he indeed was about ready to stop and go back to work, but this could only be done on the condition that, "I get one more pint to sober up on."

> **Just the word "toot" is strange. It is not listed in the dictionary with any definition pertaining to prolonged intoxication.**

Minutes later, the regular inhabitants of the local tavern were shocked to see the village preacher walk into the joint and belly his way up to the bar; the more appalling moment came when they saw him buy a pint of Corby's whiskey, slip the bottle in his coat pocket, and stroll out the door.

The next morning at 5 a.m. Fridtjof Gausen was back in school, backfiring up the furnace and emptying overflowing wastebaskets. Nothing succeeds like success, in this case with the help of Corby's. This "solution" could have made Ripley's "Believe It Or Not."

IMPORTED FROM NORWAY

NEW WOOD STOV

Made of
"Real Wood"

Sale Price Only
$39.95

GUARANTEE:
To Burn At Least 4 Hours

THE "WISDOM" FOUND IN JOURNALS

The woman who told me this story asked not to be identified, for reasons that become clear at story's end.

She crawled up to the attic once more, convinced this time that she would find that little black book. It had to be someplace up there, maybe in one of those old, dust-covered trunks pushed back in the corners, back where the spider webs covered the crumbling plastered walls, where the bats had their summer nests just inside those walls. She could sometimes hear their cheeping sounds and it made her skin crawl.

Yet finding that special book with the penciled writing would be worth the scrounging and digging through torn cardboard boxes, where mouse droppings were found between every level, every layer of half-kept, half-discarded personal reminders, be they doilies or one-piece wool underwear, or snuggies, or ancient yellowed Christmas cards. Grandpa's little black book had to be there somewhere!

Like many Norwegian-Americans, her interest in her family history came late, maybe too late. She had had every opportunity to learn about her ancestry. After all, her grandparents lived with their family when she was growing up and they had come from the old country, representing that final wave of immigrants from Norway, arriving in the early 1920s, arriving just before the new law went into effect in 1924 that reduced American immigration from a flood to a trickle.

She picked up a small printed book with the title Lesebok (Reading Book), the beginning book for learning Norse. She knew she could easily have learned the language, and her mother kept telling her–too often telling her–as much. No, she had not only dismissed the idea, but had deliberately fought it! After all, what would her high school friends say if they should find out that she was learning Norwegian? They'd laugh, and nothing cuts deeper into a kid's skin than scornful laughter. So, no way. Nothing Norwegian for her!

> ...finding that special book with the penciled writing would be worth the scrounging and digging through torn cardboard boxes, where mouse droppings were found...

She didn't even much care when her folks and grandparents spoke Norse when they didn't want her to understand something. That was all foreign stuff anyway that belonged way-back-when. That was then. This was now.

Besides, she remembered, the favorite topic the old folks talked about incessantly was the weather. Like there was nothing else that mattered every day except the weather. Sure, they were farm folks, and sure, the weather was a determining factor in their livelihood, but couldn't they, wouldn't they, please talk about something else? And the weather was never right, never ever. If it rained, then they said it was too wet; if it didn't rain, then everything was too dry. On their topic of climatic conditions, she had learned early to turn the old folks off. Click.

Then came their number two topic, the second most discussed subject, "Norwegian Ways," and how things were done better back then and there. Even as a child she reasoned that if everything was so blame wonderful in Norway, why did 800,000 + immigrants come to America? She learned to turn them off on this topic also. Click.

Despite her resistance and sometimes outright hostility, some things–really, many things–caught and got stuck in both her mind and manners. She did not realize this at the time, but gradually, little by little, and then over the years, she knew she was steeped in Norwegian culture, and then came the wonderful change of coming to love it all, to appreciate her family and want to know more and more from them. But before that metamorphosis in attitude was realized, they were gone.

Her grandparents had long been deceased. Her elderly parents she seldom saw as they, Depression children, both of them, were living the good life, which to them meant summers in the north country and winters in the sunny Southwest.

So now she was crawling around the attic, trying to find that journal that Grandpa had kept. She recalled vividly the old man opening the book up every morning after coming in from barn chores, scribbling something on those pages with a stubby pencil that he sharpened with his jackknife. There was a repeat of his writing process after the evening chores. What had he written? And where was the book?

Grandpa, she came to realize with growing amazement, had been a remarkably wise man. He also represented the stereotype of the tight-mouthed Scandinavian who said little but thought much. When once asked why he did not talk more, he replied that most people spend most of their lives never saying what they really think anyway, so why waste the motion?

After a funeral for a man who had died from cancer, he stood outside among a group of mourners who were lamenting the man's passing but at the same time congratulating themselves on their own good health.

Grandpa then said, "We are all dying." He did not mean to startle, to shock, to offend. He'd just stated what he regarded as a simple truth, so he added, "It all starts from the day you're born."

His lines brought silence from the group, who then quietly, one by one, walked away. If there's one topic those Lutherans did not want to talk about, it was their own mortality.

To Grandpa, death was part of life, which is why he celebrated the latter. He had never heard of Thoreau and his quest for the simple life, yet the old man did live deliberately, did distill the prescriptions for a calm and more meaningful life by quietly advocating the need to enjoy every day, every hour, and when something got someone into what Grandpa called "a snit," he'd say that one should then ask himself, "Will all this matter a year from now?" So he would live quietly and deliberately. Amid all the hurly-burly of daily living, he knew the secret of silence.

> **She recalled vividly the old man opening the book up every morning after coming in from barn chores, scribbling something on those pages with a stubby pencil that he sharpened with his jackknife.**

For the quiet wisdom of this man, she knew she had to find his journal because in that book there would just have to be more great epigrams, wise words expressing sound thinking with terseness and wit. His journal would be the only place where this man's deepest, most sincere but guarded opinions were stated in black and white. Indeed, it would be the highly prized journal that the board members of the Norwegian-American Historical Association would treasure and preserve. It would serve as the model discovery that all Norwegian-Americans could hope to find in their own attics.

Then she spied it! It had been hidden in the middle of a pile of old Scandinavia Co-op Creamery calendars. With shaking hands she picked it up gently and carefully opened the dog-eared cover to the first page. The search had ended, the goal reached, the Holy Grail discovered, and now she could at long last peruse the profound contents and learn the real feelings of what it was like to be an emigrant trying to make sense out of a new land, a new life, a new culture. She began to read:

"January 1. Cold again today. -22 for low and got up to zero for high. Had to use chisel to break ice in the cow tank."

"January 2. Still cold but a little better. -15 for low, 10 above for high. Looks like more snow tonight."

"January 3. Wind picked up last night. Snowdrifts need shoveling so cattle can get to water. -12 for low, -2 high."

She turned to the middle of the book and continued to read:

"April 15. Still snow in ditches and on north side of barn. Meadowlarks back. Froze again last night. Low 29, high 57."

More pages turned, more journal entries:

"August 20. Hot. Moogy out."

She recalled his made-up term "moogy" for very warm weather combined with high humidity.

"Thresh today at Peterson's. Tomorrow at Skogemoe's and day after at Thorstenson's. Might rain. Need it. Low 70, high 90."

Flipping more pages revealed only more weather reports. She placed the book back in the trunk and quietly closed the lid, then smiled to herself as she remembered Grandpa's line about how in life the dream was always better than the reality.

He was right again.

SIGN HERE!(?)

It took 135 years in America before the descendants of 2.3 million Scandinavians would unite their many Lutheran churches in 1988 and essentially merge most (not all) Scandinavian Lutherans into "one church," the Evangelical Lutheran Church in America (ELCA).

Below is a mock Application Card for ELCA Membership:

Directions: Please answer each question carefully.

Names: Thy name _____ Thy given name _____
Thy Christian name _____ Thy pagan name _____
Thy nickname _____ Thy ethnic name (if other than
Ole, Lars, Sven, or Truls; Ingeborg, Julia, Dora, Gladyce or
Christina)_____

Theology: Dost thou believe in Santa Claus? ☐   The Easter Bunny? ☐
The Tooth Fairy? ☐   Simon Legree? ☐   Reaganomics? ☐
The Preus Family? ☐   The ELCA Bishop, should he ever be a Swede? ☐
(Hope and pray for miracles.) ☐

Church Attendance: Dost thou go to church? ☐   Really? ☐
As often as they attend in Norway? ☐   (Shame on you.)
Dost thou sit in the balcony? ☐   (Shame on you.)

Stewardship: Dost thou tithe? ☐   Really? ☐   Wilst thou swear to this? ☐
List thine income_____ Now list income as reported on IRS tax form_____
Ist thou rich? ☐   Really rich? ☐   Filthy rich? ☐   How filthy?_____
Dost thou put wagers on the Green Bay Packers? ☐
Dost thou keep a strongbox? ☐   Where?_____ Combination_____

Sacraments & Training: Has thou been baptized? ☐   (Sprinkled or
immersed?) Has thou been circumlocuted? ☐
Didst thou "read" for the minister? ☐
But what did thee read: Billy Whizbang thrillers? ☐   Batman comics? ☐
Forever Amber? ☐   The Lutefisk Ghetto? ☐   Leftover Lutefisk? ☐

Leftover Lefse? ☐ Lord of the Mosquitoes? ☐ Was thou confirmed? ☐
Didst thou suffer properly through confirmation? ☐
Enough to have had to memorize and recite Luther's "Small Catechism" in
front of the whole church? ☐ You did? ☐ Wert thou scared? ☐
Didst thou wet thine pants? ☐ (If yes, thou didst truly suffer.)

The Minister: Name of congregational pastor _____
Length of pastor's sermons _____ Dost thou nod off after 20 minutes? ☐
Can anyone be saved after 20 minutes? ☐
Dost he tell "Ole and Lena" jokes? ☐ (For shame.)
Name of book from which pastor copies sermons _____
Dost thou watch the electronic church on TV? ☐
Has thou ever seen the Reverend Robert Schuller frown? ☐
Jimmy Swaggert smile? ☐ Pat Robertson ask you to vote Democratic? ☐

Home Church Policies: Ist thy church mortgage paid off? ☐
If not, dost thou still dare to serve lutefisk suppers? ☐
If served, is the paint peeling off the ceilings? ☐
Dost the odor of long dead fish served hot actually
pass through brick walls? ☐ (If yes to all questions, thou has a good
church. Smelly, but good.)

Signatures: Sign thy name ___**X**_____
Sign in Lutheran, then Greek, Latin, Aramaic, Swahili guttural and
Norwegian. If Swedish, make your usual "X."

TURNING IT AROUND: Students Are Teachers

"Brand new teachers should pay the school board for their first year of teaching because of all the things they learn."

That pronouncement was said mainly, but not totally, in jest by a retired superintendent of schools who was looking back on a career as a teacher and administrator.

True, starting teachers do learn an amazing amount that first year. You either learn fast or you don't survive! As to salary, however, well–even neophytes have their rent to pay, and they also have that bad habit of wanting to eat regularly.

As to students teaching teachers, that's also true, and the teaching can come in many areas, including how to deal with what teachers call "PANIC CRISES" and the kids call "ROUTINE RESPONSE." It was the latter important lesson that this one new teacher (myself) learned that first year, when the school board probably did deserve at least partial re-payment for the magnitude of knowledge gained from on-the-job training.

My "lesson" revolved around a tenth grade student named Jonas Malterud. Bright and eager–too eager, his cool classmates believed–he looked odd, talked odd, walked odd, and, to class members, he was odd. He was also verbally combative in that he loved to argue, often at a high pitch, with anyone who might challenge him on some point. Some students who could at times be mean-spirited would challenge Jonas, just to provoke him and get him revved up, something easily done. However, when the crescendo increased too much in volume, the students would back off because they knew something about Jonas that the teacher did not, but would learn soon.

The lesson came one day in the middle of the class period. Discussion was lively, the students were "into it," and the teacher was pleased in his role as referee between opposing opinions being voiced. When he turned around to print something on the blackboard, he heard a scuffling, shuffling noise behind him.

> In many ways it was a wonderful scene; the students knew exactly what to do and not to do about Jonas's epileptic seizures.

He turned and saw all the students getting up and moving their chairs to the sides of the room. In the middle of the open space lay Jonas Malterud, writhing and twisting, his arms flailing the air, eyes rolled up. From his open mouth emerged both grunting sounds and drool, which rolled out of the sides of his mouth. The other students weren't saying a thing.

The teacher had no idea what was going on, let alone what to do. The best he could do that instant was to stifle his gut feeling to get out of there! Obviously, the teacher's panicky look betrayed his bewilderment.

An observant student said calmly, "It's O.K., Teach. Jonas is having another fit." All the students were equally calm, not nonplused by all the commotion.

A girl added, "Yeah, he does that regularly, but don't get worried. We'll take care of him." As she spoke, a student was loosening Jonas's shirt collar for easier breathing.

The class clown then added matter-of-factly, "Jonas

comes around like that once a month, just like the meter reader."

The teacher was coming out of his own emotional panic enough to ask about the possibility of Jonas swallowing his tongue, an idea he had picked up somewhere back in sixth grade. A student more bemused by this concern than worried replied that people's tongues are rather well secured and anyone who believes otherwise is still grounded in old wives' tales. He added assurance, "Relax. He'll be all right in a few minutes."

In many ways it was a wonderful scene; the students knew exactly what to do and not to do about Jonas's epileptic seizures. To them it was common, almost routine, and it was certainly nothing to get overly excited about. They were far more adult than most adults.

In less than five minutes it was over. Jonas was sitting up and the students around him were solicitous about his every need. One had his handkerchief out and was wiping Jonas's mouth. Another brought him a drink of water. All spoke softly to him, encouraging him to "take it easy" and "take your time" and promising that "you'll be O.K."

Gradually his daze was fading and he was returning to normal. In ten minutes he was back sitting in his chair. The kids brought their own chairs back and class actually resumed. Discussion resumed also to the point where Jonas was joining in and was back receiving little gibes. Accepting challenging remarks with smiles, he seemed to enjoy returning to combat! All in all, it was to the new teacher a very strange event.

From then on the event became almost, but not quite, routine for the teacher, too. When the time came for Jonas to have another mild seizure (they occurred regardless of noise and stress), the teacher could join the class in helping and responding appropriately.

It was a great lesson learned. Kids can be bad, but they can also be wonderful!

Follow-up: This incident took place in the late 1950s, before there was medication to enable people like Jonas to control their seizures. I wish I could report a happy ending for Jonas. However, for him, for his family, the ending was tragic beyond belief. Soon after graduating from high school, he was doing well enough to gain full employment. One day, all alone, he went for a walk along a path that bordered a river. When he did not return home by dark, authorities were notified that he was missing. The next day sheriff's deputies dragged the river and found his body. Almost all believed that he had had another epileptic seizure and in that uncontrollable state he had fallen into the river and drowned.

HE THINGS THAT WERE DONE TO WEDDING CARS... OH MY!

Time was, in those years right after the war (note: "the war" to certain generations means only World War II; to this age group any other American war borders on the irrelevant) when certain semi-public events, like Saturday afternoon weddings in small town upper Midwest Lutheran churches, produced variations of mischief that entertained all —- except the bride and groom.

The wedding ceremony itself was less the immediate problem for the couple than what could – and usually did – happen right after the nuptials ended. New grooms inside tended to worry more about, and for good reason, who was outside doing what to his waiting automobile parked right there in front of the church. The varieties of possibilities were endless, and fit into certain categories:

MILDLY AMUSING. "Decorating the car" was the basic phrase denoting the need, if not the expected require-ment, of the bridal couple's friends, or alleged friends, to "Do something" to the wedding auto. And they usually did. Certain acts were obligatory, of course, like tying a string (binder twine worked well) of empty tin cans to the back bumper, the cans to drag behind and rattle and bounce noisily and happily along the road as the wedding car drove away. Often old shoes and boots were interspersed among the tied cans and if there was a metaphorical message to the shoes being there, it was long forgotten (Would she later give him the boot?).

Naturally there were thin, multicolored strips of twisted crepe paper that streamed from the front bumper, up over the hood and top of the car, and tied again to the back bumper. And naturally there were the homemade signs on the car, either taped to the vehicle or sometimes scrawled in soap or shaving lather and on occasion even whipped cream. The lines on the signs tended to be cryptic and earthy, as illustrated by the standard "Home Church Today, Hot Springs Tonight," or some crude variation thereof.

A Digression: For all weddings there was always a number of old ladies in town, of both sexes, who wrote the wedding date on their calendars, and then later, when the announcement came of the arrival of the couple's first baby, went back to their calendars and counted backwards. In this category would be a common assertion known to all as applied to the human gestation period, namely "The second baby takes nine months; the first one can come any time." (Oskar Gudmandson allowed to his crusty cronies sitting daily in front of the hardware store that there was a great potential market in designing wedding dresses for pregnant brides.)

> ...it was mischief done under the hood that produced the most vocal reactions...

MILDLY ANNOYING. When it came to "fixing up" the wedding car, it was the mischief done under the hood that produced the most vocal reactions from the happy crowd surrounding the stressed couple just prior to their departure, or planned departure. (It always seemed that the noisy crowds around the wedding cars knew what had been done and could thus sadistically enjoy more the planned misery.) Common procedures in this area were to pull off the spark plug wires so that the motor would not start. It was always good fun and lotza laughs to watch the reddening face of the frustrated groom grinding his teeth while the battery ground away at the unstarting engine. Sometimes only a few wires were pulled, thus allowing the motor to start, sort of, but to run badly, and great glee followed among the observers as they watched the tampered-with wedding car chug forward, sort of, half lurching, half stopping, half coughing and chugg-chugging along, sort of. Not an auspicious wedding-getaway.

ANNOYING. A special item of special surprise – to the wedding couple – was the attachment of a smoke bomb to the engine. When the ignition was first turned on, the bomb-sequence began, starting with an ear-piercing WHHHEEEEEeeeeeeeee whistle lasting some 30 seconds, followed by a big BOOOOM! Then came the smoke pouring out from under the hood, with some smoke rolling out from under the car and through any auto openings, totaling enough smoke to make a small cloud over the car and the hee-hawing gathering. Ohhh, the crowds loved it! Whadaway to go!? – providing the bomb had not blown away the carburetor.

DOWNRIGHT MEAN. Scandinavians saved the worst of their tricks (or best, depending on one's capacity for interpreting the Lutheran position on mankind's innate evil nature) for special people. It involved something very special: cheese. Not just plain cheese but a special (to Scandinavians) variety called Gammel Ost (translation: old cheese). This cheese was so special because it smelled so bad; indeed simply stunk to the degree that few folks could stand to be in the same room with the odor when the cheese jar was opened. Note "jar"; the runny, rheumy, slimy, greenish gobs of Gammel Ost had to be kept in a glass jar as it would otherwise eat its way through any tin container. Putrid stuff, to most folks who considered its category of cheese to be a major affront to the industry. It was Gammel Ost that made some couples' wedding days unforgettable, alas.

Consider the day Mr. and Mrs. Oddvar Thuilen emerged from the church doors, first running through a pelting rain of thrown rice on the way to their auto. Oddvar first thought it odd to glance at his new '49 Ford V-8 and see it just sitting there shiny and new, with not a single ribbon or sign or tin can attached. This seemed too good to be true! It was. They jumped in the unblemished machine, he started the purring engine, and they roared away from the church. Wonderful!

Less than two miles down the road they knew something was wrong, very wrong, very perfumy, so much so that they had to stop the car on the highway and jump out into the fresh air to avoid being sickened by the atrocious, near noxious fumes coming inside the car through the dashboard. Yes, gammel ost had been smeared all over the engine and the hotter the engine became, the stronger the smell became.

Ahhhh, the good ol'days – they were (sometimes) terrible. All in the name of fun.

(p.s. Within this wedding-car-decoration-game was the common efforts of the groom to hide his wedding car on his wedding day – using somebody else's auto at the church – and bring out his "real car" from hiding only much later when the time was safe. This game led to fervent hide-and-seek chasing by the groom's friends trying to locate the hidden vehicle and if found, perform their mischief. On a personal note, I can happily announce success in this game. Early on the morning of my wedding – in 1955!? – I brought my car, a '48 Chrysler (paid 400 bucks for it!) to our neighbor whose farm was on the edge of town and there hid it in his machine shed from searching eyes bent on its defilement. Much later, near midnight, and after the dance, the unsullied car was retrieved and away we went into the night... and into the future.)

HYMNS and HAWS

Dentist's Hymn: *Crown Him With Many Crowns*

Contractor's Hymn: *The Church's One Foundation*

Baker's Hymn: *I Need Thee Every Hour*

Optometrist's Hymn: *Open Mine Eyes, O Lord*

Tailor's Hymn: *Holy, Holy, Holy*

IRS's Hymn: *All To Thee*

Shopper's Hymn: *In The Sweet By And By*

Poor Student's Hymn: *Just As I Am Without One Plea, But That Thou Would Change My 'F' to 'D'*

Students Who Receive Incompletes Hymn: *Blest Be The 'I' That Binds*

SECTION 2:

Scandinavian-America...NOW

The Good News For Retirees:
Question: How do you like retirement?
Answer: How do you like Saturdays?

The Bad News:
Question: Didn't you used to be somebody?

Minnesota...Home of the Mispi–Mispp–
Missispp–Where the River Starts.

In Minnesota, ducks don't fly south in the
winter–people do.

In Minnesota, our governor can intimidate
your governor–and everyone else.

AS WE REMEMBER FEBRUARY: The Move To And From Minnesota

Feb. 1 *We moved to this lovely state today and for the first time experienced the snow. We had cocktails by the window and watched the soft flakes drift down. Beautiful!*

Feb. 3 *We awoke to a big, beautiful blanket of crystal white snow covering the landscape. What a fantastic sight! Every tree and shrub covered with a beautiful mantle of white. A veritable winter wonderland. I shoveled snow for the first time and I loved it! I did both our driveway and sidewalk. Later the snowplow came along and covered up our sidewalk and the front of the driveway with compacted snow from the street, so I shoveled it all again.*

Feb. 5 *It snowed 8 inches more last night and the temperature dropped to 20 degrees below zero, with a wind-chill factor of -65. I shoveled the driveway and sidewalk again. Cold out there. The snowplow came and did its trick again.*

Feb. 9 *It snowed some more last night and our cars got stuck, so I bought a 4x4 Blazer to drive in the snow and get to work. Bought snow tires for the wife's car. Jeez, they're expensive, and the ones we traded in didn't have 5,000 miles on 'em.*

Feb. 11 *Fell on my rear end on the icy driveway. Saw stars. Embarrassing. Hurt my feelings, too.*

Feb. 13 *Still below zero with icy roads that make for tough driving. Not so much fun anymore.*

Feb. 15 *Had another 10 inches of the white crap last night. More shoveling required. Just got done. And then what should come by but that snowplow!*

Feb. 17 *More snow last night. Still freezing cold. Still icy. There's now enough of it to last till August! Not pretty to look at anymore. No way. Got all bundled up to go out and shovel again (put on boots, jump suit, heavy jacket, scarf, mittens, cap with earlappers pulled down), and then I had to go to the bathroom. Disgusting!*

Feb. 20 *Yet more of that #%&@*% white stuff last night. More shoveling. And then that demon snowplow came afterward. If I ever catch that driver . . . I think he hides around the corner and waits for me to finish shoveling and then he comes flying down the street at 100 miles per hour and throws snow all over what used to be my driveway, sidewalk and lawn. Hate that guy!*

Feb. 22 *Washington's Birthday. Big deal! Bet he never shoveled snow. And last night I thought it couldn't be, but there was that stupid weatherman on TV telling us we should expect yet another 8 inches of this white junk. Does that dumb cluck know how many shovels of snow 8 inches is? Did Washington ever have to suffer once what we suffer every day? And the rumor is that dingbat snowplow driver is going to come around asking for donations, but if he comes to this house I'm gonna hit him on the head with the snow shovel!*

Feb. 25 *The nincompoop weatherman was wrong. We didn't get 8 inches—we got 10! I'm starting to go snow blind. I have a severe case of cabin fever. Even my spouse is starting to look good to me, that is when we're not arguing about some little stupid thing.*

Feb. 27 *The plumbing froze. The toilet froze. The sewer backed up. Amid the brown snow around the doors of the house is considerable yellow snow.*

Feb. 28 *The house is for sale. Arizona is waiting.*

NEITHER FORGETTING NOR FORGIVING: Time Wounds All Heels

The host exuded both fun and jocularity. Warm and outgoing, this Norwegian seemed out to erase the stereotype of the cold, stolid, down-at-the-mouth native, devoid of humor. He had visited the United States many times and had lived here a full year, moving from city to city, even coast to coast as he learned more about the banking business. His English, American style, was perfect, and he loved Scandinavian-American jokes, notably "Ole and Lena" stories, although he renamed them "Lars and Ingeborg." As a Rotarian, he had convinced his lodge in Lena, Norway, to accept its first American high school student; that student would live with three different host families during the school year, starting with his family. That student was our daughter, Karin.

The next spring we went to Norway to get her, and we were the guests of this banker and his family. He was a delightful and funny man, and we enjoyed our stay immensely. But there was one time during our visit when we witnessed a very different Norwegian banker, and inadvertently learned a dark and powerful side of Norwegian history.

Our host had driven us out to a country museum, one

of many places throughout this land where the "old Norway" can still be seen in modern times, seen in the form of buildings from the eighteenth and nineteenth centuries and some even older, buildings brought together in a kind of cluster. Bygdøy in Oslo and Maihaugen in Lillehammer are the most famous of these outdoor museums.

Still cracking jokes, our host dropped us off with the reminder that he would be back to retrieve us in the late afternoon. We walked to the entrance gate, paid our admission fees, and then were met by an elderly gentleman who said in good English that he would be our guide for the next couple of hours. That was fine and so we got the grand tour, going in and out of structures including a *stavkirke*, a very old wooden church going back to the thirteenth century; a *stabbur*, an old farm building shaped like a "V" and used mainly for storage; a big farm home once owned by a rich man (*bønder*); and a tiny farm home used by a poor man (*husman*). The tour was interesting, thanks, in part, to the commentary given by our guide, who at the end walked with us out to the road where we were to meet again with our host. It was when he drove up that the atmosphere shifted immediately from warmth and friendliness to hate and hostility.

> But there was one time during our visit when we witnessed a very different Norwegian banker, and inadvertently learned a dark and powerful side of Norwegian history.

The host was actually laughing as he got out of the car to greet us. Then he spied our guide. The two men looked at each other, neither saying a word. As the old man turned to walk away, our host said in a brusque manner, "C'mon, get in the car. Let's get out of here."

We got in but said nothing. He got in and said nothing. His drawn face was almost ashen, and he drove out in a reckless manner. We, of course, had no idea what was going on and it did not seem like the proper moment to ask.

Only after driving several miles down the road did our host again begin a conversation, at which time he apologized for his behavior and added, "But I couldn't help it. When I saw it was him, I just . . . well, I just lost it."

Apparently he read our combination of curiosity and bewilderment correctly, but he still found it hard to explain the situation calmly and rationally, though he tried. Essentially, he told us that this man, our elderly guide, was a Norwegian Nazi during World War II when Norway was occupied by German soldiers for five long years (1945 to 1950). There were many Norwegian Nazi sympathizers–too many, about 40,000–including Norwegian writer and Nobel prize winner, Knut Hamsun.

The fact that the guide that day was but a minor figure as a German sympathizer did not change a thing. He was still seen as a traitor who was not that far below the most monstrous Norwegian traitor of them all, Vidkun Quisling. Quisling was executed for his treason; only the advanced age saved the life of Hamsun, a decision pleasing but few.

Our association with this guide that day occurred over 40 years after the war had ended! But obviously, that war has not "ended"; such is the legacy and power of nationalism. Only a hint of explanation for the Americans was revealed by our host, who said simply and quietly, "You had to be here then to understand it."

Afterword: That one moment of shock-and-response-anger was the only aberration observed in our host that day or since. Our families have continued to keep in contact since we first met Leif and Grethe Skolseg in 1980. We have been to their home several times since, and they have come to America and to Minnesota to visit us in Bemidji. At Christmas each year we visited on the telephone. We last saw them in August 1997, when we visited them in their brand new home outside Oslo. Leif had retired from banking the year before, but soon afterward he got cancer. He was fighting it, he thought successfully, when we saw him in August. We knew something was very wrong when no word from him came that Christmas. A letter from his daughter in January 1998 informed us that he had only recently passed away. He shall be missed and long remembered.

Grethe and Leif Skolseg outside their new home northwest of Oslo
(Leif wearing a brace after falling off a ladder)

Ahhhh, The Good Old Days...
Actual Letters Sent To Sears
Roebuck In 1899

#1. Dear Sears Robecuk, I got the pump which I by from you but why you not send me the handle? Wats the use pump when she dona got no handle? You know he hot summer now and the wind he no blow the pump. Wit no handle wot the hell i goad to do with it? You send handle pretty quick or i send her back and order from other company.

#2. Dear Sears Roebuck, O hell. after I rite i find damn handle in the box. excuse me.

Ahhhh, The Bad Old Days...
But A Great Comeback-line

An anonymous, inebriated caller made a joking-call to the head of the Catholic nunnery, asking to speak with the Mother Superior. When she came to the telephone, the man said to her laughingly: "Hi! I'm Martin Luther."

"Oh?" she replied.

"Yup, I'm Martin Luther. Ha ha ha."

"Well, that's interesting. Where in hell are you calling from?"

Ahhhh, What might have been... Ingeborg Svensen Reinterprets The Christmas Gospel

Ingeborg asks. . . and answers: What three things would have been different if the Three Wisemen had been the Three Wisewomen traveling forth to see the newborn Christchild?

1) They would have stopped to ask directions and thus arrived in time for the birth;

2) They would have helped in the delivery.

3) They would have brought gifts that were useful.

TRUCKS, THEOLOGY, THANKS AND ENLIGHTENMENT

Background: Schoolteachers have hundreds, if not thousands, of students over a lifetime of instruction, and although the association between teacher and student may be close during those school days, seldom does that connection continue long after graduation.

One exception to the above is my ongoing communication with the Reverend James Hulberg, a Lutheran (ELCA) pastor who at this writing (1999) serves a congregation in Milbank, South Dakota. Hulberg was a high school student of mine in Osseo, Wisconsin, in the 1950s. He had a wonderful speaking voice, a "radio voice," and he was even then an excellent public speaker. He went on to graduate from St. Olaf College and from there he went to the Lutheran Seminary in St. Paul. After graduation and his ordination, he has served congregations in both Minnesota and South Dakota. Throughout his school years and career we have kept in contact, and it is the Reverend Hulberg who related to me the details of this extraordinary story below.

It did not fit. There was something wrong with the scene, this curious sight that did not jibe, this huge semi standing

74

beside the tiny church. The little white clapboard Lutheran church seemed dwarfed by this thundering 18-wheeler, its diesel engine idling noisily, making deep chortling sounds while puffs of oily smoke were being emitted from the dual exhaust pipes on each side of the shiny cab.

A young woman looked at the curious scene, shaking her head in wonderment at the two contrasting images before her. She stood a little to the side, one foot poised on the first step leading to the church entrance. She hesitated, still fascinated by this mighty machine with its multiple silver wheels, the whole outfit taking up most of the width of the narrow street.

"That's like driving a long house," she murmured to herself. "That truck is longer than the church! Amazing." And she wondered what a semi was doing here. How many block-long trucks are parked beside churches anywhere, anytime?

> Extraordinary! she thought. What strength, what power in both man and machine. Now there is a real man!

While she pondered her questions, through the door bounded a big man who took giant steps and made a half run toward the cab, there leaping easily up the metal steps and then gracefully easing his huge hulk behind the steering wheel, all this movement in one swooping motion. Then followed the harsh sounds of grinding gears, a thundering motor, and the storage-building-on-wheels eased slowly, loudly forward and lumbered down the street, like some 747 plane taxiing to take off down a runway.

As man and machine rolled noisily past the staring woman, the big, bearded driver (Paul Bunyan, he could be) waved a muscular-armed "hello." Strangely, she felt that his greeting seemed almost . . . well, personal. Then man and truck were gone.

She continued to watch, both bemused and pleased. The combined size and heartiness of both the man and his warm smile and wave were so genuine. Halfway down the block his behemoth flashed a display of red blinking lights, turned clumsily around the corner, and roared out of sight, its fading sounds altering slightly with the shifting of one gear after another, after another.

Extraordinary! she thought. *What strength, what power in both man and machine. Now there is a real man!*

A newfound respect for truckers hit her. So big, so tough, so in control. So solid and sound in mind and body. He obviously had it together! If only she could be more like that trucker.

The reverie ended and she got back to her goal, her mission inside, her resolve to meet with the pastor personally to...well, iron out some differences and make some changes. Once again she went over her arguments quickly and regrouped her thoughts for what was coming.

"Big deal," she whispered out loud, but then laughed at herself. Naw! Nope–it was a little deal, really. So minor, so inconsequential, so absolutely piddling in importance that she considered turning around and going home. After all, a Sunday school teacher's problems are pretty minor.

At the moment it seemed so silly, even sillier as she thought about her little problem, her little self, this little woman reminded of her smallness by witnessing this massive man and that gigantic Mack truck. He was doing big things, of course, and she did little things.

And yet why should she walk away? After all, that nice Pastor Hulberg was inside waiting for her to keep her appointment, and that truck business was just a noisy distraction. Shoulders back, she marched into the church office.

He rose cordially from his old captain's chair behind his cluttered desk, came around and warmly shook her hand with enough force to make her want to count her fingers afterward. A round-faced person and parson,

Reverend Hulberg was a model pastor, maybe fitting the stereotype of a proper religious leader, complete with round face, rimless glasses, bald head, black suit and white clerical collar. He simply radiated goodness and kindness and common sense.

The preliminaries were cordial but brief, the pastor allowing his need to be soon off to yet another meeting or two or three, before making a late dinner at his home in the parsonage.

"So what can I do for you?" he asked, a line that he likely repeated 44 times a week with other parishioners disgruntled with every phase of the operation, from bad hymns to bad sermons to bad potluck suppers when not enough red Jell-O salads showed up among the hot dishes.

Although she thought she had memorized her speech perfectly, she forgot it all when the moment came to say her piece, which, if nothing else, made her more sympathetic with the kids in Sunday school whom she taught in this, her first year of teaching. In fact, that was why she was there–to complain about her Sunday school teaching assignment. She had been scheduled next year to work again with first graders, the tiny tots just trying to read a sentence of three words. With this group she felt she was doing little of worth and value to anyone, herself included. She hoped she might be given kids with some advanced understanding, but no. All she taught were "The Basics," but even Biblical basics were oh-so-shallow, and so pointless. A waste of her time and energy and talents.

That was why she had asked for this meeting, to see if Pastor Hulberg would move her to more advanced work with older students, or maybe even adults, to teach people more important and concepts more important, to teach–yes, some theology. After all, she had only a year before receiving her college degree from a church-related college. She wanted to discuss eschatology, epistemology, ecumenicism–and not spend every Sunday morning as she had done the past school year showing pictures and guiding little fingers with color crayons to stay within the lines, and then sing over and over again those same three simple songs. Those awful songs. Without letup, the same, same, same songs that tiny voices loved to sing.

She could close her eyes anytime and hear those simple melodies, hear those simple words: "Jesus loves me, this I know, for the Bible tells me so." And leading teeny fingers and little arms and going through the motions of the clapping ritual on "Open, shut them, open, shut them, give a little clap." And the kids were to clap altogether, but, of course, they never did clap in unison. Useless!

Finally, the good-bye song before dismissal: "Praise Him, praise Him, all you little children, God is love." Then it was time to get their boots and mittens on, the papers sorted, the coats buttoned, and then herd them toward the door and get them aimed toward the cars of their waiting parents parked next to the church, Dad in the driver's seat reading the Sunday paper, the closest proximity to the inside of the building he got all week. A discouraging scene, as she pictured it.

Her halting words, her fumbled lines, her complaints finally came tumbling out to Pastor Hulberg, amid her too many "you know's" and the clenching and unclenching of fingers in fists. Embarrassing. But her nervous lines did come through, sort of, she thought, as she looked up at the pastor sitting there listening intently without one interruption or one raised eyebrow. She was done. Now what would he do? Or say? Would he remove her from her innocuous assignment?

He sighed. And a very long sigh it was. He leaned back, way back, tilting his old chair against the wall, his hands clasped behind his head. Then came his reply, an odd statement, or rather a question, "Did you happen to see that man who left just before you walked in?"

"You mean the truck driver? Yes, sure." Like wow, had

she *ever* seen him! *So what?*

"He's big, isn't he?"

"That's for sure," she replied. "Looked like a monstrous Viking football tackle. Powerful and strong." *But what's he getting at?*

"You're wrong on that last point," replied the pastor. "He's weak, and he'd be the first to admit it. In fact, he has admitted it to me, which is why I bring him up as an answer to your request."

"Huh?" she managed to say. It was not very articulate, but she didn't know how else to answer.

"He's a cross-country trucker. Goes all over the country, but he stops by the church regularly to drop off food that he donates. Five sacks of potatoes today. Last week it was onions and carrots. All for the church food shelf. It's his way of saying thank you."

> She wanted to discuss eschatology, epistemology, ecumenicism—and not... showing pictures and guiding little fingers with color crayons to stay within the lines, and then sing...

She stared at him, speechless.

"It comes down to this. That burly trucker thanks the church for saving his life. Well, actually he thanks the Sunday school teachers in general and . . ." The pastor swung forward to lean over the desk and look the woman right square in the eye at a distance of 2 feet. "And he really thanks you, specifically, for–yes, saving his life, albeit indirectly."

"But I don't understand . . ." This was confusing. Something strange going on here.

"He would really like to tell this to you personally but confesses that he's too shy. He doesn't know how or what to say to you, even though he said he'd try to contact you. Obviously, he hasn't. He wants you to know the whole story."

Now the young woman sat back, confused and shocked, as the pastor continued. "This is the time for what you school people call 'the teachable moment.' You're ready to learn something bigger about teaching and learning than you ever thought possible."

He sat back to explain. "A couple of months ago that truck driver was in such a state of mental despair that he really did not know what to do, where to turn. He had immense personal and financial problems, and what started as the common down-in-the-dumps feeling that we all experience at times, for him turned into major clinical depression. That's big depression. The desperateness of his situation, he told me, came to a head when he was driving his rig and winding his way down through some passes in the Rocky Mountains. At that place and moment, he said, he decided to do it. He planned to end it all right then and there, end it with the simplest maneuver of driving his loaded truck through a guardrail at some sharp curve and then fall some 300 feet to his death. Very easy to do. But he did not do it–could not do it, he told me, because of a mental picture and a voice that kept coming into his head."

On that line the pastor paused to lean forward again. "What he kept picturing was his little first-grade son sitting at home on the edge of his bed playing with his toys and singing over and over again in his squeaky voice, 'Jesus loves me, this I know, for the Bible tells me so.' The tot would then see his father and add, 'Jesus and I both love you very much, Daddy'."

Pastor Hulberg looked at the young woman. "That's it. That's all. And, of course, the trucker realized then that he could not do it, could not leave his son, could not leave his family, his home, his friends, his job, his–yes, his own life." He sat back to let the story sink in.

The young woman was stunned. She was at a loss

for words and couldn't think of a thing to say. Simply couldn't talk.

Pastor Hulberg broke her silence with a mild admonition. "From a typical alleged intellectual with a college degree, someone who's read too many books and spent too many hours wrestling with highfalutin theological concepts, teaching Christianity effectively often boils down to all of us trying to get across a few basic points, and to say those points often and say them to people early–like to little first-graders."

He was right, she now knew, but still she said nothing, just nodded in agreement. She also understood there was nothing more that needed to be said.

She stood up, smiled, and reached out to shake his hand before leaving. Without saying a word, the pastor took her hand, held it just a second longer than usual, and smiled. He knew. She knew. Then she turned and left.

Outside again, she began walking briskly homeward, feeling much better–and very different–about everything. She turned her head quickly when she heard the loud noise of a semi truck starting up from the stoplight two blocks away.

Somehow it made a different sound than she had heard before.

ADVICE TO THE LOVELORN
(back in 1915) ON 'SPOONING'

Long before Ann Landers and Dear Abby, there were those more than willing to give advice to folks seeking help, as in the case below where a Professor Shannon (he doesn't sound like a Scandinavian Lutheran) responds to a questioner wanting answers regarding this thing called "spooning". (Young readers who require a definition of "spooning" should consult their grandparents.)

Question:
"Dear Professor Shannon:

"I have been interested and worried too concerning the matter of 'spooning.' I will greatly appreciate your kindness if you will explain some things and answer some questions. Why does kissing one's sweetheart thrill him so much more with pleasure than kissing his sister? Do you think that the limited amount of 'spooning' indulged in with my sweetheart will lead to injury? Is 'spooning' a sin? How about dancing?"

Answer:
"My Dear Friend:

"In the human family, spooning belongs only to the married life. If indulged in even to a very limited extent among the single, it is fraught with gravest temptations. True love will find expression. If young people would meet each other at the marriage altar with unkissed lips, there would be no blighted lives and wrecked homes. In a man, if spooning is persisted in, it leads to sexual excitement. If spooning is continued for a few months or years, he will suffer from varicose veins. Later he may become temporarily or permanently impotent and sterile.

"In a woman, personal familiarities with men lead to troubles. The eyes that once glowed with luster will become pale and sunken. The cheeks once plump, ruddy and rosy with health will become thin and faded. Nervous prostration, invalidism, consumption [t.b.] or one or more of many other troubles will follow.

"The round dance, waltz and tango are to be condemned on the same ground as spooning. The best authorities on sex are agreed that the public dance, as executed today, has a tendency to complicate the problems of young people. But of the two, the moral hazard in spooning is far greater than dancing. Twenty fall through spooning where one falls through dancing."

RAISINS AMONG THE GRAPES: History Redone And Undone

Those who have toiled long in the Vineyards of Academia—heck, in any school house anywhere—know you don't have to look hard to find some raisins. These raisins, i.e. student-blooper-answers, show up regularly. And they're not made-up answers; no one who has ever perused a student paper or exam will ever question the goofs.

Beginning teachers become startled when they learn what their students did not learn or "learned wrong." It's all there in the exam answers. Having taught five years in senior high and three years in junior high, I believed that once I made it to college instruction, there would be no more raisins from these university "intellectuals." Wrong. Not so. At the end of my very first college lecture on Native American tribes, it seemed reasonable to give a quiz at the end of the hour. One question called for the students to simply name three American Indian tribes. Among the answers received: "The Nina," "The Pinta," and "The Santa Maria."

As suggested, new teachers are often appalled at some student responses, while older profs just sit back and enjoy them, often concluding that if David Letterman and Jay Leno wanted good comedy writers, they should hire students (except that the students didn't know they were funny). Certainly, they did not try to be funny, which makes it even better. Below are some questions and student answers off my exams which illustrate the above point:

DEFINE "THE PAPAL BULL."
ANSWER: "The papal bull was not really a bull at all; it was a cow. He was kept in the Pope's palace to furnish milk for the Pope's children."

IDENTIFICATION questions are always good for student speculation, better known as guessing. Samples:

JANE RUSSELL: "She was the wife of Pres. Harry Truman." (Perhaps at times Truman may have wished as much.)

JOHN FOSTER DULLES: "Dull, Duller, Dulles. Sect. of State who engineered some famous Packs, such as SENTO, SEETO, and NEATO."

WM. E.B. DUBOIS: "He became the first black appointed to the Supreme Court by President Horace Greeley." (If you're going to make one error, you might as well go for two.)

WALLIS WARFIELD SIMPSON: "She was an American slut who married Edward VIII, the Princ (sic) of Whales." (Some historical support for that answer.)

TITO: "He was a spy for the comunists (sic) in America."

TITO: "It was a post-war (sic) int'l plan that failed."

J. PARNELL THOMAS: "He was the Repub. candidate for President in 1948. Or maybe it was '58."

THE REV. WALTER RAUSCHENBUSCH: "A Catholic prist (sic) who believed you follow the bibble (sic)."

RAUSCHENBUSCH: "He said you're either saved or damed."

Some I.D.'s are perhaps accurate, although it's not whom the prof had in mind. Sample:

> BERNARD GOLDFINE: "This is an easy one. He was my Aunt Hazel's first husband." (Who can argue with that?)

Some student answers are so correct in a sense that it's hard to dismiss their ingenuity. Case in point:

> JAMES BYRNES: "Jimmy Byrnes was so insignificant a figure in American history that even I have forgotten who he was." (A great "answer," in that most other Americans have also forgotten who Byrnes was.) (P.S. He was first Governor of South Carolina; then U.S. Senator; next U.S. Supreme Court Associate Justice; the resigned from the Court at FDR's request to command the overall super board to supervise and run the entire homefront efforts in the second world war; then became Secretary of State under Harry Truman. Other than that he was "an insignificant figure in American History.")

"Mispelings"

Garbled spellings are always a problem. Usually the teacher can "make them out" but sometimes one wrong letter can change everything. The following is a misspelling I saw on papers for 40 years and came to look forward to it:

> *"In Europe in the eighteenth century, ten percent of the population were nobility and all the rest of the continent was composed of pheasants."* (It should have made for great hunting.)

While most incorrect spellings are perhaps amusing, there are times when a wrong letter makes for wincing disasters. Consider the identification of Cyrus McCormick whom the student identified correctly as the American who invented the reaper. However, in his spelling of that machine, he omitted the first letter "e". That changed things considerably, and he then added the unintended "information": "It did the work of a thousand men."

Scrambled Syntax

Often the spellings and definitions are correct; it's just that the phrasing is not. The results? Well, consider the student response for the definition of the WPA:

> *"The WPA was an organization in the Depression years to help men relieve themselves."*

Lines From Essay Exams

> *"The Samurai soldiers fought to their death, and if they ran, they would perform Harry Caray."*

> *"They went after Moby Dick despite the fact that they couldn't sea."*

> *"Rita Hayworth died of Old Timers disease."*

> *"I could not make heads or tales out of MCCBETH. I don't see the big deal behind Shakespear. He actually annoys me. His grammer is totally wrong."*

> *"In the book The Deer Hunter he hunts for deer and beer and other big animals.*

> *"In the Citizen Kane movie, a good example of a closeup shot is the shot of an expectator."*

> *"There are a lot of things to write about, but I can't think of anything. God, I hope I pass on this paper, I really need the grade."*

Revisionisms

How much credit should be given on some student answers that are not quite accurate, but they've gotten the general idea? To wit, a student wrote about the powerful line uttered by General Douglas MacArthur in World War II when he left the Philippines for Australia:

"Forever in American history books, young Americans will read and memorize those famous words of Doug McCarthur (sic): 'I'll be back later'."

Well, he got fairly close. Maybe it was the same person who was asked what the famous two letters were that signaled the end of the war in Europe when Nazi Germany surrendered on May 8, 1945:

"This day will forever be known as V.D. Day." (Perhaps he knew more than he should.)

Scandinavian History Students Make Their "Contributions"

BACKGROUND: Once each school year I taught a class called "Scandinavians in Amerika." That spelling in the class schedule was deliberate, hoping to draw attention to the course, but more likely it backfired, leaving readers with the impression of some dumb stereotype Nordman, and, "Dose gice can't even spell Americe, Amerrica, Aurika . . . you know what I mean."

The major requirement in the class, and the one that produced the most moans, rolled eyes and decisions to drop the course, was the mandate to WRITE YOUR FAMILY HISTORY! The outcome of this dastardly deed at semester's end for almost all the students was for them to realize this was the most useful, interesting and significant undertaking they'd ever undertaken. Hooray!

Perhaps just as important, their parents loved it and their grandparents loved it even more. Kids actually asked them–often for the first time–good, probing questions and expected good, informative answers. As an aside to both the papers and this topic, many students found out things about their background/relatives/ancestors that they were not supposed to know. "Skeletons" in the closets came out, and there was considerable calculating done on the date when babies were born in relationship to the marriage date of the parents.

While most of the family papers were very good, there were some that were . . . well, lacking (read Lugubrious; now look it up). Perhaps it was this latter group who wrote the following test answers:

What is **Stavangar**? *"An eight-stringed violin."* What does the word **Julebukk** mean? *"That's the Norwegian word for jukebox."* What is **rølepølse**? *"A very round Norwegian woman."* What is **Santa Lucia**? *"That's the Norwegian word for Santa Claus."*

Finally, an essay question asking for a ". . . lengthy paragraph on the meaning and significance of **EKOFISK**."

Explanation: Norway in the late 1960s discovered oil off its long coastline in the North Sea; Norwegians have since become "blue-eyed Arabs" and rich. As the twenty-first century begins, Norway has no national debt! They have been salting away millions of oil dollars "for a rainy day". A very prosperous nation indeed, in direct contrast to it being a poor country in the decades both before and right after World War II. Those multiple oil wells, scattered all along the coast–all the way past the Lofoten Islands above the Arctic Circle–with their huge derricks in the ocean, stand higher than the Egyptian pyramids! This whole oil thing is truly amazing, and on this topic I lectured for a full hour, with special emphasis on the first of those wells to come in, EKOFISK, located off the coast of Stavangar. Hence came the above essay exam question on the meaning and significance of EKOFISK. The resulting essay from one student consisted of three sentences. Here they are:

"Ekofisk is a Norwegian fish that repeats itself. It tastes even worse than lutefisk. Those Norwegians will eat any thing."

(In grading his exam, I added a fourth sentence, *"You will enjoy the class more the second time."*)

Headless Norseman

Advice from the Headless Norseman

Do you have trouble expressing yourself in your writing letters? If so, your worries are over. Here is an easy system of letter writing for the sophisticated person.

Most Important type — The Thank-You Note

Everyone has at one time spent Saturday night at a friend's house disastrous social gathering and this letter is designed to meet the required situation.

Dear... Today is Monday and I'm still picking the splinters from my teeth from the wood alcohol you put in the punch. One thing about your parties, there is always room for one bore. We had plenty of seafood like you said we would but I didn't think you would have to take it away from the goldfish. I'm enclosing a used stomach pump for your other guests to use also.

Burpingly yours,

Surprise Gift

Writing a letter in return for a surprise gift is the second most important type.

Dear.... You don't know how surprised I was when I opened your large package this morning and found a full grown alligator! It's just what I've always... imagined. Why already he has eaten the family dog and taken a big chunk out of the mailman's leg. Where did you teach him such cute tricks?

Surprisingly yours,

Popping the Big Question

A letter asking a lady's hand in matrimony is most difficult to write. One tends to be too direct and thus reveal his stress and anxiousness. Thus one should always be nonchalant about popping the question.

Dear...How are you? I am fine. I hope that you are fine too. The weather is nice. Sometimes it's not nice. The humming-birds are humming, the thrushes are thrashing and the robins are robbing. How is the corn crop in Iowa. Does your grand-mother still have athletes-feet? Will you marry me? Have they hanged your brother yet?

Disingenuously yours,

Strive to Be Witty in Job Applications

In writing a letter asking for a job, one should strive to be as jovial as possible because a boss just loves to have a sagacious employee around to keep the other drones from doing their work.

Dear... In answer to your ad for a good bookkeeper. I should fill the job perfectly since I have kept every book I ever bor-rowed. Yak, Yak, Yak. As for my description, I'm eight feet tall. You see I was sent up river for a long stretch. Yuk, Yuk, Yuk. My western friends call me Bicarbonate because I was one of the first settlers. Yacuk, Yacuk, Yacuk. As for references, my folks are in the Iron and Steel business. My mother irons and my father steals. Oh Yakul, Yakul, Yakul.

Howlingly yours,

WHEN PLANNING HAS NOTHING TO DO WITH LEARNING

They sidled into the classroom, blathering away to each other in twos and threes, with side comments and insults to their friends already there, most sulking as they slid into their assigned seats. After all, it was just another routine day of school, another day to be endured rather than enjoyed.

What was the topic Mr. Blekestad had scheduled for the day? Oh, yeah. Progressivism. Teddy Roosevelt and Woody Wilson and that gang. Boring. And who cares? The subject held about as much fascination as that poopy picture of George Washington hanging above the blackboard. George floating on clouds, or so it looked. George with the bad teeth–or was it no teeth at all? No wonder he didn't smile, the old wuss. Definitely uncool.

There, writing–no, PRINTING BIG on the blackboard was Mr. Blekestad (Mr. Fat Stuff, Lardo, Porcine Paul–behind his back), printing his saying-for-the-day, "VISITORS? YES. COMPETITORS? YES. ENEMIES? NO." Only the class air heads would miss that one, what with their arch enemy coming to play a game Friday night. Lines on a blackboard would hardly prevent the expected fights. Cool.

So another day, another hour to survive. Ho hum. Bummer. Then came a surprise—more than that, a shock. The bell had just rung and Mr. Blekestad had gone to shut the door when in walked Eric Olson, but not the Eric the kids had known last spring, the classmate who did not even start school in the fall because he was sick and fighting cancer. Now Eric was back for the first time and he looked...well, not only awful, he just looked weird. A walking skeleton.

Eric hesitated at the doorway, knowing Mr. Blekestad's rule about wearing caps, and removed his baseball cap, revealing total baldness. His skin wasn't even close to pink or tan. It was milky white. Hospital white. Had his face been immersed in flour, it would not have seemed more ghostlike—and scary weird.

The chattering stopped immediately as Eric slinked into a chair. Around him others not very subtly began to move their own chairs away from him. A leper wearing a sign UNCLEAN! could not have been less welcomed. Yeah, they felt sorry for him—but just stay far away, please. Cancer is not supposed to be catching, but you never know.

> Now Eric was back for the first time and he looked...well, not only awful, he just looked weird. A walking skeleton.

Mr. Blekestad sized up the situation and knew both what not to do and what to do. The former involved a planned lecture on Wilson's New Nationalism; the latter involved an unplanned lesson on cancer, so he said, "Eric, it's great to have you back again. It's been a while since we've seen you and...well, out of curiosity, would you kind of fill us in a little on what's been happening in your life?"

Eric looked up with his big blue eyes, which were looking even bigger against his white skin. He hesitated, then looked down again, apparently hoping Mr. Blekestad would leave him alone and go on to some other topic, but the teacher came back quietly and rephrased the request. He could see the curious looks on the faces of the rest of the class. They were ready.

So Eric began talking–rather, mumbling–so that a voice from the back row hollered, "Hey, Eric! Stand up and go up front, so we can hear you." Again, the hesitation, but again, the smile of encouragement as the teacher motioned Eric to come forward.

Eric started to explain some things and the more he talked, the more the student class leaned forward to listen. Eric told them about fatigue and listlessness, about sores and strange lumps, then the trips to the doctors' offices, and then faraway trips to Mayo Clinic specialists–and all those x-rays. Then the radiation treatments. Then worse, the chemotherapy, the dreaded chemo. The chemo that destroyed the cancer but left the body devastated, sick beyond description.

"Often you pray to God to let you die," he said. "There's the vomiting. The just plain puke and more puke 'till there's nothing left to come up but your guts, but you still spew the phlegm and mucus–the viscous material secreted as a protective lubricant coating by glands in the mucus membrane. Add to that the outside lesions and the ugly red splotches all over . . ."

The class sat spellbound, not one soul making a face, let alone coming forth with an adolescent "Yuck!"

Eric continued on about welcomed cards and letters, the visits by pals, the support of his family, the anger and screaming frustration of his dad who wanted so much to do anything he could to help him but was left helpless. And then there was the love without letup of his mom, and how just her touching him made him feel better as she sat beside him day after day, months at a time.

Lastly, Eric told them about remission. And hope. And

prayer. And uncertainty–the odds in one's favor, the odds against. And how happy he was just to be alive.

To the surprise of everyone, Eric had rambled on the entire period. He looked up at the wall clock and said, "Well, that's about it."

More silence. Eric stood there uncertain what to do.

Then a girl popped up and said it for all of them. "Eric, I learned more about cancer today in 50 minutes than I have in my lifetime." She got up and walked toward him. "Y'know what I feel like doing now? I want to give you a big hug." And she did.

Her friend who sat beside her said, "Me, too." And she did.

Then came more "me, too's." At that moment the bell rang, ending the period, but instead of rushing out the door, students had formed a line and one by one the entire class gave the slightly bewildered Eric the best coming-back-to-school present he could ever hope for.

Mr. Blekestad, at the end of the line, shook Eric's hand and said, "Thanks for the best history lesson that will be taught for a long time."

Eric mumbled something about not understanding, but at that moment two boys had grabbed him, one by each arm and were hauling him off, pushing and shoving, to their next class, Eric smiling now and the friends laughing as they lurched through the hallway door.

Mr. Blekestad was smiling, too, realizing that truth of what the ed-psych books about teaching had called "the teachable moment." It had been a great unplanned lesson.

Postscript: Although there were name changes above, the story is true. And it may come as no surprise that the teacher was, a couple of years later, chosen as the State Teacher of the Year. "Eric Olson" also lives on. He's apparently a healthy young adult at this writing (1999).

TRUE (?) STORIES

Perceptions.

The late Minnesota Governor Karl Rolvaag loved to tell the story of the Pennsylvania Quaker farmer and his mean cow, Matilda. It seems that one night the farmer sat down to milk Matilda—and the cow kicked the pail over. He retrieved the spilled pail, sat down beside Matilda once again—and the cow gave him a wet-tail-swipe across his face. Nevertheless, once again the Quaker farmer started milking and this time Matilda kicked him and sent him flying against the wall. At this point the farmer got up and walked to the front of the cow-stanchion, looked Matilda right in the eye, and said: "Matilda, thou knowest I cannot curse thee because I am a Quaker. And Matilda, thou knowest that I cannot strike thee because I am a Quaker. But, Matilda, thou knowest not that I SHALL SELL THEE TO SOME MINNESOTA LUTHERAN FARMER WHO SHALL POUND THE HELL OUT OF THEE!"

Fatal Warning...

As senior citizen Lars Trulson was driving down the busy freeway, his car phone rang. His wife Ingeborg was on the line and she said, "Lars, I just heard on the radio news that there's a car going the wrong way down the freeway! Please be careful, then."

"Holy Moses!" replied Lars, "Its not just one car, there are hundreds of them!"

The Lutheran-Catholic Debate Goes On...

Truls Larson lived next door to Paddy Murphy. Truls sees that Mr. Murphy took him to the Catholic Church on Friday nights to play bingo, but they called out the numbers in Latin so the Lutheran couldn't win. They later got into a big argument about who was the more knowledgeable, a Priest or a Pastor, with Paddy finally blurting out: "Our Catholic Priest knows more than your Lutheran Minister!" To which Truls replied: "He should. After all you tell him everything."

The Lutheran-Lutheran 'Debate' Goes On...

Four Lutheran Pastors wanting to get better acquainted met over coffee and eventually, though unplanned, they ended up making confessions to each other, the first one saying sheepishly that he had actually taken some money out of the offering plate. The second then averred that his great sin was drinking too much communion-wine after services. The third Pastor, emboldened by the others, then admitted to having lust in his heart for certain women in his congregation. The fourth Pastor had listened very intently to the others, then announced with anxiousness: "My great passion and sin has always been to spread gossip and rumors..and I can hardly wait to get out of here!"

"NEVER TRUST A SKINNY COOK"

Background: It all began with a class discussion on the long-term effects of World War II on American soldiers. After class, a student came up to me and said with half amusement that his dad was a vet, and he would get up in the middle of the night and fry himself a hamburger. "Sometimes he eats a lot more than a burger," he added. "Ya, and we've got a sign hanging in our kitchen that says NEVER TRUST A SKINNY COOK."

That kind of peculiar information can arouse curiosity. What aging adult awakens in the wee hours of the morning and prepares himself a full meal? Something's strange here, something worth investigating. Next came phone calls, a brief visit with the wife and her demurrals as to her husband's willingness to talk about his painful war experiences, but finally his agreement to be interviewed. The answer to the "night food question" was not at all surprising. Indeed, it made perfect sense–and is a moving story with a message to every American.

Biographical sketch

Clyde Statton was born on July 8, 1925, in Cumberland (Barron County), Wisconsin, the son of William and Mabel Statton. Clyde was one of 11 children (seven boys, four girls), and number eight in the order of birth. His parents were farmers in Wisconsin but lost their farm in the Depression. The family moved to Bemidji, Minnesota, in 1938, to locate on another farm about 7 miles north of town.

The mother of that large family had been a hotel cook prior to her marriage and was both a good cook and one used to cooking for large numbers. Of their economic circumstances in the Depression, Clyde would recall, "We were poor but didn't know it because we were on a farm where we had a big garden and had plenty to eat."

Clyde had begun elementary school in Wisconsin, but at age thirteen moved with his parents to Bemidji where he finished the eighth grade at Northern Elementary School, a rural school located about 5 miles north of town. Following graduation, he lived at home but he went to work at D&H Machine Company in Bemidji for $12 a month, where he became a machinist.

A neighbor told him, however, that he should instead be attending high school, saying, "Get your hind end back in school!" Otherwise, he could expect to get drafted into the United States Army. Clyde ignored this advice. (Eventually six of the seven Statton brothers were drafted into military service.)

Soon after his eighteenth birthday, Clyde was drafted into the United States Army in August 1943. He first went by bus to Fort Snelling, Minnesota, to receive his physical. The bus of draftees from Beltrami County was full, with the majority of the men being eighteen and nineteen, but there were also some men in their thirties who were fathers. The need for more men in the military was acute at that time, so when asked if physical problems kept many of them out, Clyde said, "If you could raise your hand, you were in."

Clyde was first sent to Camp Walters, Texas (southwest of Fort Worth), for 17 weeks of basic training to become an infantryman. Not tall (5 feet 8 inches), he weighed 150 lbs.

when he went into the Army and was in good health. He indicated that he was fed well during basic training and gained weight during that time, so that he weighed about 170 lbs. when he was shipped overseas the next spring of 1944. He was assigned to the 94th Division in the 3rd American Army, that army under the command of General George Patton. Clyde both saw and heard General Patton once, describing him as "a dirty-talking man."

Clyde received $50 a month as a private. His pay went up $10 more when he trained for and received the Combat Infantry Badge, and an additional $10 was added for overseas duty. His entire division (16,000 men) left together on a single large ship, the *Queen Elizabeth*. Leaving from New York and traveling a fast 30 to 35 knots, the ship arrived and landed in Scotland three and one-half days later. Their landing in Scotland was a second choice. England was first because enemy submarines were sighted. The men went by train to southern England and soon his entire division went in together from England to France, landing on the beaches at Cherbourg in LST boats in late July 1944. The first Normandy invasion had been the month before on June 6, so the landing beaches had been secured by the time Clyde's division landed.

His division was soon split in half; part went one way and the other half another. Clyde's unit was assigned to the Western Front in Luxembourg. The primary fighting line then was located between the German Siegfried Line of Defense and the old French Maginot Line. Here his combat days began and he remained on the front lines for the next seven months until he was captured by German soldiers in January 1945. He remembers that day as though it were yesterday.

On January 20, 1945, it was intensely cold outside, about 15 to 20 degrees below zero. Clyde and his squad were then holed up in a recently captured German bunker and were being shelled that morning by the Germans.

Several of his buddies were killed, including Clyde's best friend, and many other Americans in the bunker were wounded by the attacks. Only about a half dozen men were alive when they were instructed to surrender or all be killed. (An American soldier who spoke German was able to communicate with the enemy soldier who gave the order.) The few Americans left talked it over and the men decided to surrender, about 11 a.m., coming out of the bunker with their hands up. Clyde had an unhealed broken wrist caused by an earlier fall–not by artillery or rifle fire.

> ...the men received one slice of bread every other day (six men had to divide one small loaf); their other food was one small bowl of soup made mainly of flour and water, given every other day.

Upon surrendering, their first orders were to help carry wounded German soldiers back for medical help. Second orders were to carry back the dead German soldiers in the area. After that, they were ordered to carry out from the bunker the dead American soldiers and lay them in rows. (Clyde believes that these bodies were later recovered by the American troops who retook that same bunker a few days later.) Lastly, they were ordered to clean up the bunker so that the Germans could return to use it again.

Clyde and his fellow American captives kept moving back day by day with the retreating German army. Along the route, all Americans captured were interrogated one by one for about an hour by an English-speaking German. The Germans were seeking special military information, but Clyde said as a private he had no special information that he could have given them anyway. Officially, all captured soldiers were to tell only their names, ranks and serial numbers. All this time the captured Americans were never allowed to stay overnight in either a tent or a building, they were given almost nothing to eat, and they slept outside in the snow each night without being given any covering. The common name they were constantly called by their German captors was Schweinhund ("pig-dog").

On their way to a P.O.W. camp, the Americans one day were ordered to march into a small German country schoolhouse and were held there for several hours. Inside the school a large picture of Adolph Hitler was hanging on the wall. One American turned the picture around. When the German soldiers came back later and saw Hitler's picture turned to the wall, they became very angry and demanded to know who did it! When no one confessed, several soldiers raised their machine guns, pointed them at the Americans and announced that they would all be killed right then and there. At that point, one American stepped forward to say he did it. He was then taken outside and was never again seen nor heard.

Finally, the remaining Americans were brought to a German "prisoner of war reception center" with the curious name of Camp Lindbergh. Near that camp they, along with other American prisoners, worked both on repairing a railroad track and improving an athletic field, this location near Frankfurt. However, this area was then bombed by American planes and Clyde received shrapnel wounds in both legs from one bombing when he could not get to a shelter in time. Neither the shrapnel wounds nor his broken arm were ever treated; the wounds had to heal by themselves.

Clyde still remembered his German-assigned serial number: #96302. He was sent to a P.O.W. camp called, in German, a Stalag. Clyde's Stalag number was 9-B. It was a camp with about 3,000 American prisoners and 3,000 men from other armies. There was a fence between the two groups. He was assigned to a barracks with approximately 50 other men. There were no beds, no furniture, and everyone slept on the floor. Each was assigned one blanket. The men often slept four to a grouping so that four blankets would cover them in the freezing night temperatures. There were no toilets and, of course, no toilet paper, only a hole in the ground outside with a log across it; that served as their latrine. This P.O.W. camp was Clyde's "home" for the next 74 days.

The Americans in the camp were separated into different barracks by rank; that is, privates together, corporals together, and the like.

> Those P.O.W.s who could manage to stay alive also suffered from trench foot, caused by the cold, dampness and constant wet feet.

"You didn't know anyone," said Clyde, "and didn't necessarily trust anyone either, even if they were fellow Americans. Besides that," he added, "guards with guns were everywhere. When you're looking down a German gun barrel every day, you're always worried–and afraid. Damn right, you're afraid!"

For food, the men received one slice of bread every other day (six men had to divide one small loaf); their other food was one small bowl of soup made mainly of flour and water, given every other day. Nor was there any water available to drink–the men ate snow for liquid. On occasion, one man would steal another man's food, especially if one left a piece of bread lying unguarded. Adding to their awful conditions was their worry of either stool pigeons among them or American-talking Germans who were "planted" amid the prisoners to snoop and try to gain inside information about any secret American plans.

Obviously, their lack of food and nutrition made all the prisoners weak and they lost much weight. Clyde went from 170 lbs. to less than 100 lbs. in his 74 days there. He said, "Two guys I knew died from starvation."

Many others in their weakened condition easily became sick, and just as easily died. "For the living," Clyde added, "we all had diarrhea or dysentery, of course."

There was also just plain boredom. "There was nothing to do within the Stalag fences. No activities, no nuthin'. We just sat there hour after hour, not talking to nobody." Clyde added that one of the few diversions happening almost daily was helping to carry out the bodies of the newly dead, hauling the corpses outside the gate where the living American P.O.W.'s then dug a shallow grave. Each body was carried out in a homemade box, the corpse dumped into the grave, and the box then brought back inside the compound to be reused for the next body.

Those P.O.W.'s who could manage to stay alive also suffered from trench foot, caused by the cold, dampness and constant wet feet. Many men lost toes and part of their feet. Clyde also added that even when men were not sick, "We were all just crawling with lice."

Things improved a little in March of '45 because the weather began to get warmer. Best yet, by the end of the month the prisoners could hear cannon fire in the distance and knew the Americans were advancing closer every day.

The great day of liberation came for Clyde Statton and his fellow prisoners on April 2, 1945, when an American army unit came and freed them. By that time most of the regular German soldiers had retreated, but the German guards around the camp–"Men in their sixties," said Clyde–stayed and surrendered as they were glad to get out of the war any way they could. The liberating American soldiers did not want to get close to the American P.O.W.'s because, ". . .we were all lousy. They didn't want to touch us."

With liberation, the prisoners were given their first real food, army C-rations, and they loved it! Inside the kitchen were found great quantities of that "soup" the men had received every other day, but the liberators inspected it, found it unfit for human consumption, and threw it all away.

Within hours following their freedom, all the ex-P.O.W.'s were marched first into a "field shower" to get clean, receiving their first shower in many months (and for some, a year or more). The showering was followed by a "delousing," after which each man received a new set of clothes, none of which fit because they were all so emaciated. Their old clothes were tossed together into a pile and burned.

The ex-prisoners were next flown to LaHavre, France, to a reception center there for former P.O.W.'s, which the men called "Camp Lucky Strike." Before the men got on the planes, because each had major bowel problems not under control, each G.I. was given his own five-gallon pail and a full roll of toilet paper.

In the days, weeks and even months following their liberation, "Food was the only thing we thought of," said Clyde. For example, the men got in the chow lines to receive their platter of food, but after they finished eating, they immediately got back at the end of the line and went through it again, and again. ("Sometimes the waits in the chow lines were an hour or more, so we were hungry again by then," added Clyde, now smiling.)

In preparation for their returning to the United States, all the former prisoners were assigned in groups of eight to ten to an officer whose job was to literally bring each of his men all the way back from France to their homes in America. In mid-April, Clyde and fellow ex-prisoners got on a ship for America for a three-week voyage to New York; they arrived on May 2, 1945. (On their way over they learned of the death of President Franklin Roosevelt on April 25. Soon after they landed, they rejoiced in the announcement of Germany's surrender on May 8.) On that voyage, the ship's baker said he baked more bread in three weeks than he had baked the entire previous year! By the end of the voyage, Clyde was up to 115 lbs.

In New York, the men took a troop train west, with Clyde and his officer-guide getting off at Minneapolis and then going on to Fort Snelling. Because he had been a P.O.W., Clyde was told that his discharge from the army would come soon; ex-P.O.W.'s were automatically to be discharged. For this reason and at this time and place (now back in Minnesota) he chose not to apply either for a promotion or for a Purple Heart, even though he was eligible for both. Clyde Statton simply wanted out and home, then and there.

Despite not yet having official furlough papers (they caught up with him later), Clyde took the train from Minneapolis to Bemidji, arriving about 4 a.m., but with no one to meet him, he walked immediately from the depot to the nearby Third Street Cafe. Although he had been told by army officials that his parents had been informed of everything that had happened to him, this was not true. All his folks knew was a single telegram informing them that their son was "missing in action." Not another word to them about the P.O.W. camp and the April liberation. In the cafe, Clyde met an older man he had known before and this man, at first surprised to see him and then appalled to see how skinny Clyde was, called Clyde's father, who immediately came to get him. It was one joyful reunion for Private Clyde Statton and his family! Eventually Clyde's five brothers in the military all came home alive, although two of them had been wounded.

That July of '45, Clyde received orders to report to what the army called a "convalescent camp" in Arkansas. "That camp," laughed Clyde, "was the kind of army I liked." The men were treated royally and the food, lots of it, was great. While most of the men stayed three weeks, Clyde was allowed to stay six. When he left he was up to 175 lbs.

From Arkansas he was sent to a California National Guard camp where his work was minimal and the food was maximal. At this place his weight went up to 200 lbs., and he knew it was time to cut back on his eating. He did, and he began to lose weight. While in California, he was also officially discharged from the United States Army in November of 1945, and he returned to Bemidji. As a civilian again, he went back to the same place he had left two years before, back to D&H Machine Company.

Several other jobs would follow over the years. For example, he worked for Otter Tail Power Company for 20 years. Eventually Clyde set up his own businesses, operating both a small lumber company and a meat processing plant appropriately called "Statton Meat Service." His home and businesses in the country are located only a couple of miles from the farm he and his parents moved to back in 1938. In 1948, Clyde married Lois Gregg; they would have five children, three boys and two girls.

> **On that voyage, the ship's baker said he baked more bread in three weeks than he had baked the entire previous year!**

At the close of the interview on December 13, 1997, Clyde Statton was asked how he felt about his special wartime experiences, now over 50 years ago. After a long and thoughtful pause, his response came:

"Those memories never leave me. My first years back, those things never used to bother me, but they bother me now...it's hard to talk about. I realize how close I was to dying and (pause) there were those many brave guys who did die. Some things are hard to talk about, even now. (Long pause) There's not enough money in the world to buy that experience, but I wouldn't want to wish it on anybody. I don't believe I could ever get through it again. It changes you. It changed me, not for the better."

Although his old division, the 94th, has had several reunions since the war, Clyde has never attended any of them. He said, "I used to check the list of names of those planning to come, but I never knew any of them, so I didn't bother to go."

Only recently has Clyde started going to a veterans hospital in Fargo to be part of a follow-up program on the lives of American World War II P.O.W.'s. There he learned that well over 90 percent of those P.O.W.'s have had heart problems. He was also examined by doctors and was told that he had had a small heart attack himself, likely occurring when he was a prisoner in that German *Stalag*.

–End of interview.–

Across the table sat this aging but healthy, rugged-looking man with a round, ruddy face, a man who obviously spent a lot of time outdoors. His large, rough hands were those of a strong working man, one who easily threw around both slabs of lumber and slabs of meat. At that moment, he was smiling and his eyes were lit with mirth. He was happy because finally the interview was over, all those probing questions over, and the often painful responses and painful memories of being a prisoner of war over–but surviving.

It was now both simple and clear why, during these last 50 + years he would frequently get up in the middle of the night and fix something to eat. It was BECAUSE HE COULD! He was a free man. He knew what freedom meant. He also knew what brought that freedom.

For Clyde Statton, World War II is not over.

Clyde as a soldier (1943)

Clyde today (1999)

All you wanted to know about lutefisk, and then some...

LUTEFISK WAS ONCE A DISH FIT FOR KINGS AND PRINCES

"Mr. Fixit" in the Minneapolis Star-Tribune came to aid of readers curious about the origin and value of lutefisk.

Question: My Scandinavian friends laugh when they talk about lutefisk, yet I believe they eat it. I don't get it. Lutefisk is not a fish as far as I know. What is the story behind lutefisk?

Answer: Many people consider lutefisk second-class food, which is why the often-maligned fish product and the people who eat it frequently are the target of jokes and ridicule. But according to the Institute of Nutrition in Bergen, Norway, it is more nutritious than any other type of fish!

Lutefisk, literally meaning "lye fish," is dried cod that has been soaked in lye. Originally, the solution was made from birch ashes. Treating fish with lye breaks down the protein chains and amino acids of high quality are created during soaking.

While the origin of lutefisk is a topic for debate, Norwegians have been eating it since the Middle Ages, according to Norwegian ethnologist Astri Riddervold. A fish rescued from the water and ashes after a fish yard fire in Norway might have been the first lutefisk to be eaten.

Whatever the origin, lutefisk has been considered a delicacy since it has been around. It is easy to digest and chew, which may explain its popularity in the Middle Ages when dentures were rare. Also many people at that time believed that fresh fish was hazardous to one's health.

Lutefisk was considered a dish fit for kings and princes in Norway and Sweden in the 1500s. It became part of the Christmas food traditions in those countries, so today when people serve lutefisk during the holidays, they continue a practice started by their Scandinavian ancestors.

There are several ways to serve lutefisk — with melted butter, cream sauce, or with any other toppings. It was the same in the Middle Ages when individual households prepared the reconstituted cod according to their preference.

As for the jokes, lutefisk is often the butt of jokes, but primarily in the U.S. In Norway a lutefisk joke would be considered about as funny as a tuna-salad joke told here.

Lutefisk is no joke to the Olsen Fish Company in Minneapolis, believed to be the world's largest producers of lutefisk, but you might find some jokes in Minneapolis author Greg Legwold's "The Last Word On Lutefisk." The book includes facts, fiction and folklore surround the fish.

"In Cod we trust."

"Lutefisk, the Cod that passeth all understanding."

PROPER MANNERS?
You Are Also How You Eat

America Versus Norway–
At The Dinner Table

"You are what you eat" is an old familiar line that's often applied to particular foods connected to particular ethnic groups. American children indirectly learn their heritage by the foods that are served to them, with the greatest learning taking place at Christmastime, the season when ethnic dishes come forward on the table in abundance.

"You are how you eat" is a less familiar line, but it, too, indicates heritage. For example, the basic use of knife and fork while eating meals in America is standard procedure that is seldom thought much about–until one realizes all folks don't eat that same way.

Americans dining out are made aware of the differences when they see European tourists eating at the table next to them. Some Americans are amazed; others are amused as they watch someone holding the knife in the right hand, the fork in the left hand, and neither being shifted from one hand to the other during the entire meal.

Europeans are equally amazed and amused at the American practice of constantly shifting the fork and knife back and forth during a meal, and they regard the constant motion as a strange waste of both time and effort.

An added instance of how foreigners eat can be observed by watching a Norwegian visitor receiving an American breakfast of coffee, toast and two fried eggs. When the food arrives and the waitress has departed, the toast is placed on the bottom of the plate and the eggs are placed on top of the toast. At that point, the breakfast moves bite by bite from plate to mouth by way of knife and fork. The food is not touched by the hands. To Norwegians that is simply the proper way to proceed. Any other way is simply . . . well, improper.

Norwegians and Americans differ in what they label a "sandwich." In Norway, there is never a second slice of bread on top. They speak of open-faced sandwiches, which aren't sandwiches at all, at least as Americans know them. Even for the Americans in Oslo who eat sandwiches with their fingers, there may be the advantage of seeing what they eat. No surprises lurking between two slices of pumpernickel!

The above description and explanations are necessary in order to tell a true story of a dramatic culture clash between the United States and Norway. Thanks to the Rotary Club, our daughter spent a year in a Norwegian high school as a Rotary Exchange Student. Near the end of her stay, her host family suggested that she prepare a strictly American meal for her school friends before leaving. After all, they had said, she spent the year eating Norwegian foods; now it was time for Norwegian teenage girls to experience eating American foods. In thinking about what to prepare, she took little time in concluding that there is little more that is American than a plain hamburger.

The feast day arrived. The food was prepared, the girls were in attendance, and there lying on the plate before each guest was a steaming hot, big, fat, juicy hamburger, the sides hanging over the bottom of the bun. The girls looked strangely at this large, round concoction, and they looked back and forth at each other, not knowing what to do, how to proceed. At that moment our daughter stood up to give a demonstration. She reached for the ketchup, took the top off the bun, and poured on a generous supply of ketchup over the hamburger before replacing the top of the bun.

"And this is how you eat a hamburger," she said. "You grab it with both hands, bring it up to your mouth, and bite off a big bite." Which she then proceeded to do.

The attentive young women watched closely with great curiosity bordering on fascination. Again they all looked at each other, and without anyone saying a single word, each one removed the top of the bun and placed it on the side of the plate. Then they each picked up a knife in their right hand and a fork in their left hand and proceeded to carve away at their American hamburger, now converted into an open-faced sandwich.

A proper reaction to culture shock? After all, you are *how* you eat.

(Picture of the American–our daughter, Karin–is in the book Leftover Lefse.*)*

114

A "PRAYER"–OF SORTS– FOR TOURISTS!!

Heavenly Father, look down on Your humble tourists who travel this earth walking around in their drip-dry underwear, wearing goofy hats, with cameras slung over shoulders, and carrying arms full of schlocky souvenirs and mailing postcards that don't arrive until we're already back home.

We beseech You that our bus be on time–that all our group members be on time–that we receive our very own baggage at each stop.

We pray that the phones work, that the operators speak our language, and that there is no mail from our children at the next hotel causing us to cancel the rest of the trip.

Give us strength to visit those endless museums and churches and cathedrals, but if we skip historic monuments to take a nap after lunch, have mercy on us for our flesh is weak. (And after five cathedrals, they all start looking the same anyway.) Protect the wives from bargains they cannot afford. Lead them not into temptation for they know not what they do–or buy.

Keep the husbands from looking at strange women and comparing them to their wives. And perhaps put bras on those endowed younger women who walk by and cause husbands' heads to swivel sharply enough for whiplash. Save the men from making fools of themselves, and please do not forgive them their trespasses for they know exactly what they do.

And when our tour is over, grant us the favor of finding someone who will look at our home movies and watch our slides and listen to our endless stories. We ask this in the name of Best Westerns, Ramada Inns, three-star hotels, and our local travel agency whose lying brochures got us going in the first place.

WHEN THE "MALL OF AMERIKA" MOVES TO MINOT

You have to see it to believe it. Some 60,000 people, all milling about under one roof at the state fairgrounds in Minot, North Dakota, most having driven hundreds of miles to get there. Many come from distant states and Canada to be part of the state's biggest social bash of the year. They arrive via cars, buses, motorcycles and R.V.'s, their vehicles filling up the vast parking lots before the drivers and passengers can wind their way to the main entrance and join the throngs herding slowly through the multiple turnstiles. Got to get inside and see . . .

See what? What's going on? Why are all those people there? And why are the motels and hotels within a radius of 100 miles booked five years ahead for folks who want to get to Minot in mid-October? For Norsk Høstfest, of course, which answer probably makes little sense–unless one is Scandinavian! Then, Minot in the fall becomes Mecca.

Høstfest is the Norwegian term for "Harvest" or "Fall Festival." It's a four-day event billed a "Scandinavian Festival" to celebrate heritage, that is part show, part circus, part fracas, part sales, part nostalgia–but mainly social and mainly fun, if expensive. There is indeed a feeling of warmth and friendliness that permeates this mass gathering, even for the many husbands who get dragged along reluctantly. For some folks it's a return to yesteryear and the perceived "good ol' days" on display in sight and sound all around. Norsk Høstfest officially emphasizes Scandinavian heritage in general and Norwegian culture in particular, even if buttons are sold there reading "100 Percent German–And Proud of It". To this, most onlookers say, "Wiedersehen."

Although the hype of big-name entertainers brought in for the main stage are hardly Scandinavian (Bill Cosby comes to mind), once the hordes of people get through the doors, it's strictly all-Scandinavian. All the dozens, perhaps hundreds, of booths and the bazaars and the bands and the foods are required to have some Scandinavian connection. And they do. So inside it's Scandophile heaven, be it the availability of delicious rømegrøt, or Hardangar embroidery, or Icelandic prune pudding, or Swedish Darlana horses, or Danish appleskiver. And, of course, lutefisk and lefse. Ah, Viking nirvana under metal roofs!

For some folks it's a return to yesteryear and the perceived "good ol' days" on display in sight and sound all around.

In each of the several buildings, a couple the size of large airplane hangars, there's something different to see and hear, and the sellout crowds shuffle slowly from one building to another all day long. In one massive room, for example, are long, multi-aisles for shoppers, with little "stores" on either side. This becomes a temporary Viking "Mall of Amerika," with merchants (mainly amateurs) selling almost everything imaginable that is Scandinavian. To illustrate, in one corner you can see two Finns finishing off logs and constructing a log cabin as you watch, and then afterward you can buy it! And, of course, there are Norwegian sweaters and more sweaters, and rosemaled wooden plates and more plates among artifacts seemingly available by the thousands.

And then back in another corner of this Viking vastness

is "The Authors' Table," a section set aside for authors of books, which must have Scandinavian themes, of course, to peddle their wares while seated on cold metal folding chairs, their published works stacked in piles in front of them. Given the massive numbers of potential customers coming by, who often stop for a look-see at the covers and contents, the chances for book sales are considerable–yeah, mouth-watering–and therein lies the subject of the rest of this tale,

"Goliath Versus David-son in a Literary Non-Battle".

Selling books at Høstfest is by invitation only. My first time there at The Authors' Table was most memorable, because of what did not happen.

An explanation, of sorts. At the first table–the best table, the table on the corner that everyone had to pass–sat a special author, a renowned national scholar, a man of such academic credentials as to have been chosen chairman of two big-time university Scandinavian studies departments, first at the University of Wisconsin and then at Harvard. He published profusely in scholarly journals; moreover, he wrote literary biographies and books on literary criticism and college textbooks, and he had even edited and written the standard Norwegian-American dictionary. He was in demand to give addresses at national and international conventions, and he had enough degrees and letters after his name to fill the alphabet. Indeed, he was A Big Man. And a big man physically, too. His books are equally big in size. Certainly, an impressive figure in background and publications and appearance. His book sales should have been tremendous!

At the other end, at the last table–the worst table, the table easiest to avoid–sat a little man, a man small in stature, with his academic credentials the same size. After a summer of attendance at a state "normal" school, he became a one-room country schoolteacher in rural North Dakota, and years later, after graduating from Concordia College in Moorhead, a high school English teacher in a northwestern Minnesota town, his location at the time of his recent retirement. What he wrote and published throughout his teaching career were little, sometimes tiny books that were most unscholarly. He published in no esoteric journals and he gave no speeches at national conventions. Indeed, he was A Small Man. An unimpressive man in appearance and background and academic publications. His book sales should have been minimal.

> At the other end, at the last table—the worst table, the table easiest to avoid—sat a little man, a man small in stature, with his academic credentials the same size.

This little former country schoolteacher had to compete with this big Harvard University professor for book sales. Not fair. No contest!

It was no contest, all right, but not the outcome that might be expected. The little man outsold the big man 100 to 1. The winner's name was Erling Rolfsrud, and he should have gotten writer's cramp from all his autograph signing! People had to stand in long lines before him, waiting patiently for their turn to buy a book, to meet him, to shake his hand, to introduce themselves or introduce a family member or two who had also read some of his 28 books, and they obviously loved both the little books and the little man. It was an amazing scene, and we watched with wonder and fascination.

It was so much more than just cold book sales for Rolfsrud. For him there were regular hugs and steady pats on his shoulder and occasionally a kiss planted on his cheek, and all the offered physical affections. His responses to them were so genuinely bestowed and received as to suggest that every book reader of his was essentially a fellow family member. Extraordinary! And a beautiful sight to witness, a genuine display of warmth and humanity on the part of all involved. And the buyers were indeed involved in the writings of Erling Rolfsrud, the son of immigrant parents from Norway, the author who wrote about life as they knew it and understood it. He was truly one of them.

Obviously, Rolfsrud had informed and entertained–yes, enthralled three generations of readers, and hundreds of those same patrons now had the opportunity to meet him personally, to thank him personally–and yes, by their actions, to honor him personally, and at the same time scoop up his latest book.

It was a unique scene for an outsider (myself) to witness. Certainly, it could restore anyone's faith in humanity. Here was this modest figure who sought no special laurels but yet in full public view was receiving constant praise and thanks and well-pumping handshakes from readers, the words of praise sometimes projected at considerable volume. (As a Norwegian-American, Rolfsrud said later that it was "kind'a embarrassing" to be a recipient of such open affection.) Genuinely grateful people queued up to wait their turn to say directly in sincere, if simple, ways their warmest "thank you's," and by the same token to say indirectly that they loved this kind, gentle, elderly man who wrote readable books.

His fans came in all sizes, shapes and ages to wait their turn. Many carried old, beat-up books he'd published 35 years ago, readers at last getting the chance to get their dog-eared editions signed on tattered flyleaves. Some mothers had children in their arms and hanging onto their legs, but those little limbs got disentangled long enough for the moms to make sure they'd shake the hand of Mr. Rolfsrud.

In this repeated scene came the oft-repeated line, "Remember, kids, those wonderful stories I read to you that you liked so much? Well, here's the man who wrote 'em. Yes! Yup, kids, there he is—right there. See?"

And they saw. And they believed. And then followed Mom's second line, "We've got all your books and read 'em over and over again."

Amid the mob of admirers, the gracious Rolfsrud never faltered in his total interest in each person before him, regardless of age. Once he reached in his pocket to give a little boy a couple of bucks; the lad was short on cash to buy a book.

Frequently, the person approaching him would begin loudly with the words, "Well, then, Mr. Rolfsrud, you remember me. Of course, you do." And, of course, he didn't, but he never let on to any memory lapse, and guilelessly sought out clues in their conversation that might jog his memory enough to come up with a close enough approximation of name or title for the recipient to beam satisfaction that convinced him that, sure 'nuff, that nice Mr. Rolfsrud remembered him after all. Sure he did. You betcha! There were a few close calls, like the fat, red-faced, bib-overalled and exasperated farmer who finally blurted out that he was Alfred Johnson. And the quick-thinking Rolfsrud jumped in to say that, of course, he knew he was a Johnson—but just didn't quite know which Johnson, at the moment.

> **Amid the mob of admirers, the gracious Rolfsrud never faltered in his total interest in each person before him, regardless of age.**

You betcha the authorities who ran Høstfest also knew of Rolfsrud's reputation, and more—and had done something about it. He was officially named to their Hall of Fame that year, a special honor complete with banquet, medallion-and-ribbon and a plaque. Rolfsrud alone would notice that his name was misspelled on the plaque and later observe wryly that this could only happen by and to a Norwegian, but he never mentioned the misspelling to the authorities. Typical Norwegian!

So much for the "literary contest," of sorts, at a Høstfest Scandinavian orgy, of sorts. David–or Erling–triumphed over Goliath. No contest. It was a victory for humanity.

Afterword: When returning from Minot, I was still so impressed (perhaps "moved" would be the better word) by the Rolfsrud recognition that I wanted to share it with others, and so I wrote up an article that appeared in the Bemidji Pioneer *Newspaper.*

A couple of weeks later I received a postcard from Rolfsrud, which read, "A Bemidji friend (from college days) sent me a clipping of your Pioneer article about the Høstfest and me. You were most generous and kind in your appraisal of me! At times I laughed so hard that the tears came and I had to stop reading. Mange takk. *Also, generous orders for my books resulted because of your article. All's well here (retirement in Farwell, Minnesota). Had so much fun recently on a Fargo-Moorhead radio talk show that the co-hosts want me back. Ya, you betcha, ve vuss talkin' 'bout Norvegians! Sincerely, Erling Rolfsrud."*

(See Rolfsrud picture, on the next page, sporting his medallion, seated at The Writers' Table at HØSTFEST. Rolfsrud passed away in 1994. His books, however, are still available, handled by Caragana Press, 910 NW 9 Street, Grand Rapids, Minnesota 55744, or call the dealer at 1-800-494-9124.)

Rolfsrud sporting has medallion at The Writers' Table at HØSTFEST

SCANDINAVIAN LAWS
OF THE UNIVERSE

Nostalgia isn't what it used to be.

It's hard to be nostalgic when you can't remember anything.

All things being equal, fat people use more soap.

No matter where you are, there you are.

Things may seem as bad as they can get but don't bet on it.

By the time you make ends meet, they move the ends.

The other line always moves faster until you get into it.

If you think there is good in everybody, you haven't met everybody.

Anything is possible if you don't know what you're talking about.

Everybody lies, but it doesn't matter since nobody is listening anyway.

Cleanliness is next to impossible.

If the shoe fits, it's ugly.

A closed mouth gathers no feet.

When the going gets tough, everyone leaves.

Friends may come and go but enemies accumulate.

The secret to success is sincerity. Once you can fake that, you've got it made.

Happiness is merely the remission—or transmission— of pain.

For every action there is an equal and opposite criticism.

Never attribute to malice that which is adequately explained by stupidity.

The world gets a little better each day and worse in the evening.

Trust everybody, but cut the cards.

Any noun can be verbed.

History doesn't repeat itself, historians just repeat each other.

People who love sausage and respect the law should never watch either one being made.

TWO SPECIAL VIETNAM WAR VETERANS

Introduction: Teaching in a college in the 1970s meant having many Vietnam War vets attend school. Of all those whom I got to know, two stood out, not for what happened to them in Vietnam as much as what occurred when they became returning college students.

Manny Beck

His name was Manny Beck. He had grown up on a farm north of Bemidji with his parents and his grandfather, Manfred, for whom he was named. When he returned from the war–actually from the veteran's hospital–and just before starting college, he married his high school girlfriend. The newlyweds lived in a rented farmhouse near his parents' home.

Manny stood out in a curious sense because he was so quiet. He spoke only when spoken to, answering softly and laconically. He was unlike his fellow vets, who usually hung around together and not too subtly made it clear that they were indeed war veterans, and he avoided them. In class he sat alone, sitting ramrod straight in his classroom chair, a position so unlike those of his slumped-over classmates. Alert, never missing a word, he sucked up information like the proverbial sponge.

The chance of getting to know Manny well (does anybody really know anybody?) seemed especially unlikely, but because I served as his advisor he had to see me regularly and privately, and he had to talk if he ever hoped to complete all the paperwork required for graduation. Only then, in my office, very gradually and in tiny increments of information, did enough of his experiences in Vietnam come out over four years' time–enough to give at best a semi-picture of what had happened and the added difficulties before him–even if he graduated with straight "A's," which he almost did.

In Vietnam, Manny was a squad leader whose small unit was attacked suddenly one night by an overwhelming force of what he called "the North Vietnamese Liberation Army"–all that! So formal, so technically correct, but so different from what most veterans called the enemy, which ranged from "Vietcong" to "Charlie" to "Black 'Jama Gooks" to the normal "V.C." In this attack, Manny was severely wounded; he still has the mortar fragments in his body. His major wound, however, was to his head, and doctors had had to insert a steel plate inside.

Although his recovery was painful and very slow, it appeared complete except for one major exception, his sense of balance. He had none. Although his legs were fine, he had to learn to walk all over again, and after a month in a vet's hospital, he had mastered it. The only way Manny could walk straight, or even stand up, was for him to look intently out in front of him; that is, to look at the "horizon," that which was level. In effect, if he could see, he could walk. If he could not see, he could not walk.

Manny was philosophical about his plight. He was thankful just to be alive. He was not bitter, not angry. He did not hate the North Vietnamese, nor was he ever in opposition to the American army being there. He did admit to American naiveté–he actually called it "stupidity"–about our understanding of South Vietnam politics. But overall, he believed American goals were desirable, if not honorable. Asked if he'd go again, he said, "Yes. If your country calls you, it is your duty to go." For all of the above, he was a very different kind of college student.

When his classes ended in the afternoon, he would walk to a designated, if somewhat remote, spot near the football field where his wife would be waiting in the car to pick him up. All went well until this one day in January. The days were short–precious daylight short–and the day was cold, very cold. The ferocity of the Minnesota winter had taken its annual grip. It was not just brisk cold, but brutally cold. The minus zero temperature that is not weather jokes cold (the kind that makes the national network news that people in short-sleeved shirts in the South laugh about), but dangerously cold (the kind that numbs exposed limbs in only two minutes). The kind of cold that can kill you.

Dusk was fading fast when Manny left the building. Delayed after class and knowing the urgency of the time, Manny hurried as fast as he could to make it, using a different route. He couldn't do it.

After my last class, I went back to my office for some last minute stuff prior to heading home for supper. It was to be the regular ritual, the same route to the car in the parking lot where the same grinding down of the battery began before the engine would catch the spark and grudgingly the motor would operate, one reluctant cylinder after another. For reasons not known then nor now, I took a different route that day.

Outside, the cold was palpable. Spit froze before hitting the ground. At that late hour the campus was deserted. Not a soul around. Desolate, and so cold. Looking over the distant library, the smoke from the chimney was hanging low, forming a descending gray blanket that spread over the roof–a clear sign of intense cold when smoke will not rise into the sky.

As I trudged along the packed snow, so cold that each step made squeaking sounds, the enveloping murky twilight had shifted silently to darkness, and along this empty path it was suddenly startling to make out a figure ahead of me. He was lying on the ground, then getting up, then falling down and writhing, then trying to stand again but soon falling, never making a sound. As I got closer, it appeared to be someone totally intoxicated, some falling-down drunk trying to make it home. There is an urge to avoid such people, an internal message telling you to cross the street at that point, or at least not to look at them while you scurry fast around them.

> **He was lying on the ground, then getting up, then falling down and writhing, then trying to stand again but soon falling, never making a sound.**

I planned to do the latter, though I intended to take a peek at this disgraceful figure while hurrying by. The fallen man was, of course, Manny. He was as surprised as I, but this was no time to linger and talk. He took my extended arm, rose to stand, and like the blind man he was under those circumstances, walked with me the remaining 100 yards to the car and to his worried wife, who was on the verge of hysteria. She was getting ready to leave the car to go find him along the usual route, which he did not use that day.

Afterword: The above event is rife with "what if's," but they become pointless in the way it turned out. Manny turned out all right, too. After trying teaching for a couple of years, he decided what he really wanted to do was farm. And he did, and he does.

Roger Olafson

His name was Roger Olafson. He was an ex-Marine, an angry ex-Marine who had done two stints in Vietnam, the second one at his own request. From California originally, he ended up in northern Minnesota and college because he had liked the area, having visited some shirttail relatives in Minnesota when he was a child.

He was a big, burly man, with tattoos on both arms. He always rolled his shirtsleeves up so that all could see a large eagle on one arm and the Latin *Sempen Fidelus*. On his other arm was the American flag and the inscription DEATH BEFORE DISHONOR. It was the latter term that brought on his anger, he believing that there was no honor left in America in general and certainly none around the colleges where all the draft dodgers had come to avoid military service.

He had been married and divorced twice, acknowledging openly that both his drug addiction ("a little souvenir from Nam," as he phrased it) and his alcoholism ("got that stateside") were the causes. He added that he believed both were under control, if not behind him, thanks to an earlier stay in a V.A. hospital, and currently to the special vets' counseling center and his weekly sessions there in group therapy. "We end up hollering a lot but I guess it does us some good," he said, adding, "We're a crazy bunch, still."

In class, he sat in the front row in the very end seat, and partly because of this proximity, we often visited before my class lecture started. It was during those brief encounters that gradually his anger toward his male classmates, whom he disdained to sit near, came out on a regular basis.

"The biggest group of yellow-bellies our nation has ever put up with. Wimps, all! They don't know what real men are like. We did our duty. We went and fought and loved it! Strong and brave, that was us. Not crybabies like these–these dinks!" His further comments were only a variation on the same theme.

Thus it came as little surprise that he asked if he could talk to the entire class when we got to the subject of the Vietnam War. He said he wanted to tell it like it was, make it clear how they should be proud of the strong and brave G.I.'s who fought for their country, so that freedom might have been brought to South Vietnam.

"No namby-pambies went there. The media sold us out." He simply bristled with ferocity when he got on the subject of war, and I felt hesitancy about allowing him to give what would likely be a harangue. Regardless, his viewpoint was in the minority as by then conventional wisdom had gradually become that the United States had made a monstrous mistake in sending some 57,000 Americans to their deaths in Vietnam–for nothing. However, with a view to letting the class hear the other side, it was agreed. He could talk, bark, bellow, scream, hurl insults to the class, and use the entire period, as he requested.

> Standing on the raised platform in front made his 6 feet 4 inch hulking frame appear even bigger.

The day arrived. In preparation, a large map of Vietnam was displayed, big enough to cover a third of the blackboard. Roger Olafson wore his old Marine fatigues that day. The sleeves on his shirt were rolled up so that no one would miss the tattoos on his muscular arms. Standing on the raised platform in front made his 6 feet 4 inch hulking frame appear even bigger.

He began with a voice that could be heard in the next county. "Let me tell you college kids what war is really like," he shouted, "but first I'll show you where hell-on-earth is located!" He went to the map, his finger moving around as he looked for certain places.

Some apparent confusion occurred as he kept looking at the map and not saying anything. Just his steady staring seemed to trigger something in his mind because when he finally began to talk again, the volume had been reduced by half. He started to describe in some detail a fire fight south of Hue for him "and my fellow grunts" and how only a few of them were rescued from certain death by an evacuation helicopter that miraculously got in just in time to get them out.

Again he hesitated, then looked down, and appeared to be in deep thought about something. A long wait. Members of the class began looking at each other, some with quizzical faces, and a few began rolling their eyes.

When he finally began to talk again, his voice started to crack. "A lot of my buddies didn't make it back that day," he said quietly.

Another pause. "Jeez, we got hit hard," he added almost offhandedly. By then we could see the eyes welling up.

"My best buddy–hell, we'd been together since basic training at Paris Island. Him they put in a body bag, one part at a time. Gonna send him home in pieces. Gawd, that was awful! Maybe had I been beside him, I could'a saved him."

By now he was not trying to address anybody. He was at best rambling, with one unrelated line following another.

"Like, y'know, when a guy beside you takes a bullet in the head, it makes a kind'a squishy sound, like the round goin' through a watermelon or sumpin'."

Another pause.

"Hey, man, it was bad. I'll never forget it!"

Pause. Then tears dribbled down his cheeks, and all he could get out of his mouth was, "Those poor bastards. Jesus, it really gets to you."

Pause.

"Day after day of God-awful heat, and all that killing. And you di'n't know who the hell was the enemy. All them gooks all around you, some friendly, most not. Hell, they hated us! Even little kids had grenades they'd slip in our tents!"

Pause.

"Nuthin' changed except the hit list. Soon nobody left of the guys you knew. All gone, all dead. For nuthin'. And we were all strung out on drugs just to try to keep sane. By '72 a whole army disintegrated. Hell, we wuz fraggin' our own officers at the end! Crazy."

At this point he was not able to control his grief, and the hulking young man put his face against the blackboard and began to sob, his thick shoulders heaving up and down. He then glanced at me and gave a little wave.

The message was clear. He was done.

Another little waving motion was given to the students, who got up and filed quietly out the door ten minutes after class had started. In a major way, however, it had been a "full" class period. It was the best "lecture" on the effects of war that could ever have been given.

And no one there that day would ever forget it.

Afterword: Roger Olafson came by my office that same afternoon and was a very subdued figure. He was embarrassed.

"I dunno what got into me. I just–y'know–just find it hard to talk about . . . jeez, I'm sorry." Only when it was pointed out to him then how totally effective his talk was in ways he never had in mind did he feel better about his abortive appearance before the class. When he left the office, his final line likely said more about him and his future than either of us knew: "I'm a mess."

And he was. He did manage to stick out the rest of the school year, but then he dropped out of school and left town. I never heard from him or about him since. For him and all the other Rogers who were veterans of the Vietnam War, there will always be those invisible scars to plague them. Good soldiers. Bad war.

I WANNA GO HOME

Parents hope that their children will grow up to have good memories of their childhood; and what better memories can or should there be than their recalling with nostalgic fondness their father taking them out in the woods at Christmas time to get the family Christmas tree? (As it turned out, their better memories will have to come from some other event). It seemed like a great idea at the time - to the father,. Get the three kids together, drive out in the country, take along a sled for a magic ride along a magic snowtrail; take an ax along to chop down that perfect tree that the kids would pick out, and on the happy journey homeward in their comfy car, together they'd sing some happy Christmas carols as the happy family meandered its merry way back home. Didn't quite turn out that way.

The challenge on that designated day began with below zero weather, but the greater challenge followed with all three kids saying collectively and individually that they'd rather not go. The high school boy said it was boring; the middle school daughter said she wanted to stay home and telephone her friends; the elementary school girl was engrossed in another "Little House on the Prairie" book and wanted to stay home and finish it.

What to do? Christmas was closing in. The father then appealed to all three, with no success; he then cajoled them, with no success; finally in desperation, he demanded they go! After all, this was going to be family fun!

With that kind of persuasion, the reluctant kids were stuffed grudgingly together into the family "73" Volkswagen Beetle and they were on their way. Hardly had the car turned onto the main road before came a declarative sentence from middle school daughter: " I wanna go home."

Strange how such a happy family going off to get a Christmas tree can be so silent in a tiny car. The only uttered lines for the first 10 miles were variations of the refrain, "I wanna go home."

Finally the magic woods was reached. The car stopped and the brood tumbled out and then just stood there. The big boy said " I'm bored"; the little one said "I'm cold"; the middle one said "I wanna go home."

The father, with his sudden hearing loss, got the big sled out and made the magnanimous gesture to pull all three down the frozen logging road. The boy said he wouldn't be caught dead sitting on a dumb sled with his dumb sisters, the middle one cried "I wanna go home." But the little one accepted the offer and hopped on the sled; the alleged happy family thus plunged into the woods.

> **The big boy said "I'm bored"; the little one said "I'm cold"; the middle one said "I wanna go home."**

They at last came upon a nice spruce tree with great possibilities for the living room. Would family consensus now be reached on said tree? "Should we take this one?" asked the father. The son said "I dun' care"; the mid one said "I wanna go home"; the small one said No, "I want a prettier tree than that".

So forward they trudged, on and on, the penetrating cold persisting, the grumbling persisting. Another stop: "How 'bout this tree? It's very pretty." "I dun' care." "I wanna go home." "I want a prettier tree than that."

Back along the frozen trail, back to find the prettiest tree in the forest. Then backward off the sled fell the little one and she rolled into a snowbank, getting snow in the face, and worse, getting snow up the sleeves of her coat. Variations of speech patterns followed. "This is, y'know, like dumb." "I really wanna go home. "I'm really cold."

So followed a reluctant turn around. More slipping and sliding and mumbling grumbling as they turned back. And darkness was descending, along with the temperature. Action with the ax was called for forthwith and thus a near approximation to a Christmas tree was felled, with no vote allowed as to its degree of prettiness. "Well, good! We have our own tree. Don't fight now but which of you would like to pull our Christmas tree out of the woods?" "Not me. Oh for boring." "I wanna go home." "I'm freezing."

Back to the car came the Frozen Four. Back down the return road they started. Old VW Beetles had poor heating systems; it took a mile or more for them to heat up inside. The temp inside had just become close to livable when it happened. The plastic windshield-fluid container under the dashboard burst suddenly, first sending sprays of blue liquid over shocked faces, and then flooding the floorboard. But even worse was the strong smell; the stench was almost overpowering and to get fresh air, the windows simply had to be opened - at 20 below zero - at 55 mph.

It was not a good ride home, but it was a memorable one. Down the frozen highway bumped the wounded, stinking Beetle and inside the cold and strangely silent (numb?) figures said nothing, but by then all four had the same idea in mind: "I wanna go home."

Addendum

Now a generation later, the "kids" are grown; the two girls are married and have children of their own. They remember the above event well and smile - although not a very big smile - when they recall the incident. And they seem to have "learned from history;" learned not to repeat history's mistakes.

WHEN THE MESSENGER GETS THE MESSAGE

Having this major interest in all things Scandinavian in general and Norwegian in particular has led this writer to accepting a considerable number of speaking engagements. I even got asked to talk (twice!) at the American-Swedish Institute in "Minnaplis, then." No Swede jokes allowed, however.

Whatever the major focus of the speech, as requested by the host group, I'd always slip in the importance of family history, even quoting a line from Isaiah, where he tells all to "Know ye the rock from which thou wert hewn. . ." This emphasis on families recording their heritage on paper, and nowadays on tape or film, became a near obsession. I'd preach with missionary fervor on this need, appealing to the audience's sense of guilt if they had not yet done their family history. And with all those Lutheran listeners out there, laying a guilt trip was easy.

A line that seemed to strike a chord was a rhetorical question: "Haven't you said to yourself that you should go and talk to Great Aunt So-and-So in the retirement or nursing home? She knows more about your family than anyone. Then before you make the visit, she passes away, and the family history that she could have added to is gone forever! Boo hoo."

Another recurrent theme about family history in my talks included more rhetorical questions, after which almost all there nodded their heads in agreement. The questions: "Have you not at some time looked at an old photograph of people and been very curious as to who they were? And then turned over that same picture to find nothing written on the back?"

Then followed my missionary message: "Take every family picture you own, get a soft-point pen, and on the back of the picture print clearly the THREE W's: Who (giving first and last names, not just 'Uncle Truls'), When (the date/year), and Where (where the picture was taken). The reward for your efforts is to leave an important, lasting history for your children and grandchildren."

> The reward for your efforts is to leave an important, lasting history for your children and grandchildren

Encouraging audience members to complete the "picture identification needs" was normally well accepted. Although I have no scientific evidence to prove as much, there were enough folks who contacted me later to say they had actually done it.

Encouraging audience members to write their own family histories was another matter, however, and likely one that failed more than it succeeded. A special appeal would be made to grandparents and their need to inform their grandchildren that they were not born grandparents at all, that they were actually young once themselves. So write it down for them! As reasonable as this sounds, it was and is hard for many grandparents to write anything except their names on the back of their Social Security checks, alas. But there are shortcuts that are still useful, namely what's called "grandparent books," small, almost pamphlet-sized publications found in most bookstores. In these "books" the writer simply answers/responds to the questions asked about the person's early life. The result is a quasi autobiography that is still important to young and old family members alike. Just do it!

Now, finally, to the message in the headline to this story. My talks reached full passion only when I got to the MESSAGE on the MANDATORY NEED for everyone to leave a written record to/for his/her family. I brought along one prop. Given its size and weight, I'd slip it into my back pocket just before going up to the podium, and at the right dramatic moment (well, the speaker thought so), I'd haul it out and wave it back and forth (the waving motions alone woke up the dreamers).

The prop was a homemade, handmade, large chisel. It was a crudely made implement, not smooth metal (lots of bumps), pounded out on an anvil by my immigrant grandfather, Lars Lee. After the waving came my line, "This was all he left!"

Dramatic pause. Despite a little Norwegian fudging in that line–actually I have his wedding ring and a pocket watch he brought from Norway, one that winds with a key–the MESSAGE was true that he left no written records of his life. No journal, no autobiography, essentially no family history. Just the dumb chisel.

Then my power-blow sermon to the audience: "Years from now do you want someone standing before a group, waving some artifact of yours around, telling them that you left no written history of yourself? Of your family? For shame!" (A great guilt line.)

My talk concluded on that point, with a throwaway line that I always used when I gave talks in southern Minnesota: "And remember this warning: Never buy fresh fish from the back of a pickup truck with an Iowa license plate." Then I'd sit down.

It was after one of these talks that the importance rather than the unimportance of that chisel was brought out. An audience discussion once followed in which an elderly woman stood up to say that she thought the chisel was "a wonderful and important symbol that, by itself, summarized this man's life."

Huh? What's this all about? She then asked her fellow audience members, suddenly attentive, "If each of us were to leave one and only one thing for our family that basically summarized our life, summarized who and what we are–a single artifact that they'd later see and then say, 'Sure, that's it'–what would that one thing be?"

Her question got everybody there thinking, talking and speculating. A lively discussion followed, which included a group analysis of Grandpa's chisel and what could be deducted just from that one implement.

Sample questions: "Was he not a self-made man? A self-learner? Likely a farmer, physically strong? An independent soul? A jack-of-all-trades, one who was required to live simply and frugally on a pioneering small farm, which semi-subsistence farm and farmer-produced almost everything they ate and drank?"

Answers: "Yes." "Yes." "Yes," to all the questions.

The messenger received the message.

Now, readers, if you were to leave your family members just one thing . . . what would it be?

Providing Information On Scandinavian-America:

CHANGING PATTERNS OF HISTORICAL WRITINGS

Preface:

There are many ways to define History and not all are complimentary. I once had a perplexed college student who defined history as "one damn thing after another." He has a lot of company. Moreover, there are some big-name cynics who have supplied their own interpretations, like Will Rogers who observed that "History ain't' what really happened; it's just what historians tell you happened." Perhaps the ultimate in cynical comment comes from Voltaire: "History is tricks that the living play on the dead."

Alas for all of the above. The goal of history should be positive and honorable; history writings should follow the definition of history as stated by the late, great historian Carl Becker: "Knowledge of things said and done." That simple; yet really that difficult.

Warning:

Before getting rolling on Scandinavian history, there are a couple of big but necessary terms to make clear, namely Bibliography and Historiography (those words have made potential history-majors switch to math; the terms can also cause book browsers to quickly put this book back on the shelf). A bibliography—bib for short—is simply a compilation, a listing of books and articles written on a subject, in our case a bib on Scandinavian America. Historiography, however, is the changing, shifting styles and interpretations given to those same writings. (See, that wasn't so bad.)

Getting Closer:

Obviously the Scandinavians to and in America provided a rich legacy; their histories needed to be written and many were, so bibliographies began early and continue to grow as more keeps getting written and published every year. Thus by 2000 there are fat bibs on Scandinavians in general as well as semi-fat bibs on each specific ethnic group. Now of special note and interest (well, to some folks) comes that word Historiography, the "ways" those multi- histories came to be written.

Ready, Set, Go:

Scandinavian historiography falls into three periods and patterns, starting with:

1. Gathering and Preserving the Documents (1870s and 1880s)

As early as 1847 Norwegian-American newspaper editors began appealing to their readers to save and bring in their old diaries, journals, letters; keep those church records and the township records too; and hang on to those musty-smelling black books for later perusals, those old records that lie in piles down in the basements of the court houses. But who will take them, take care of them, preserve them? Answer: The Scandinavian-sponsored church colleges. For the Norskies in the Midwest, it would be Saint Olaf and Luther and Augsburg and Augustana and Concordia— and others— who became the repositories for preserving the solid documentation necessary for later sound, solid historical writings. (sidenote: on an exam I once gave, I asked for the definition of "repository"; one student wrote instead the meaning of "suppository." Yes, life is confusing at times.)

2. Efforts of Amateur Historians to Interpret the Past (1890s-1920s)

The histories written in this early time period tended to be written by amateurs, gifted amateurs maybe (mainly clergymen, also newspaper editors), but persons both motivated and articulate enough to get the stories down on paper and later published as books, booklets, pamphlets (is that smaller than a booklet?), and articles. The major critcism of these early writers was their basic tendency to be. . . well. . . get ready. . . "fileo-pietistic." Uff da.

There it is—fileo-pietistic. It means, well. . .it means essentially "laying it on t'ick," the tendency of the writers to tell only the good and omit the bad; to give interpretations that are at best questionable (Did those Norsk immigrants really come by boat or did they walk across the water?); where every single soul to Amerika was a flaming success, e.g. Truls Larson's sons all went to Yale! (or was that jail?); each newcomer just automatically, genetically became a paragon of virtue (not a single sinner in da whole blame bunch, den!). Perhaps all this is appealing to believe, but it's simply not true.

Illustrative of another aspect of the early writings can be noted by a book published on OUTSTANDING NORWEGIANS IN AMERICA. Guess how many were women? Answer: none. (p.s. What does Uncle Torleif call "a man out standing in his field?" Answer: a farmer.)

#3. Professionals Organize Professional Societies (since1925)

On the centenial anniversary of the first Norwegians to America, 1925, professional historians and writers met together at Saint Olaf College in Northfield, Minnesota, and there and then founded the Norwegian American Historical Society. Two of the biggest names—and first officers of NAHA—were Ole Rolvaag and Theodore Blegen. Rolvaag taught at Saint Olaf; Blegen the Dean of the Graduate School, University of Minnesota.

The somewhat curious complimentary term for the publications coming out of NAHA was that their histories included"warts and all." In the phrasing of a more modern cliche, "they told it like it is"—or was, and have been "telling it" honestly in some 100 published NAHA books since its formation.

(It should also honestly be stated that both Swedish-Americans and Danish-Americans have excellent historical societies, again closely connected with their church colleges.)

And then a group for all Scandinavians. While SAS is well known to Americans as Scandinavian Airlines System, less known is SASS, the Society for the Advancement of Scandinavian Studies, founded in 1928, an organization of academics dedicated to scholarly studies that include all five Scandinavian coutries.

Conclusion/comment:

"Dey done good, den."

WHERE WE'VE BEEN, HOW WE GOT THERE. WHERE ARE WE GOING?

A popular book called <u>Passages</u> lays out the pattern of change for individuals over a long lifetime. However, there was also a pattern of change for immigrant communities over a long lifetime.

Regardless of their emigrant origin country–Norway, France, Czechoslovakia, Belgium–or whether those new-comers went to live together in a section of a large city or in a small rural community, the evolutionary changes over 50 years for that particular ethnic group in America became essentially the same. Indeed, there were four basic stages–four headings–that cover those passages: (1) **Getting There**, (2) **Setting Up the Community**, (3) **The Community Matures**, (4) **Decline and Survival**.

Not only were there four basic patterns of changes, but also in each category occurred the same fundamental assimilation and Americanization problems along this bumpy road which led to their becoming present-day Americans.

To follow through the four step pattern, let us take, for example, some of the earliest Norwegians-to-Amerika (who else even spelled the country wrong/right?) and place them arbitrarily in the time period from 1900 to 1950.

(Astute readers have already said to themselves correctly, "This writer is making many generalizations, to which the proper historian's sneaky reply is, 'Yes, but generalizations are generally true'." If the reader can grudgingly go along with that premise, we can proceed to follow that four-step process in "the rise and fall" of ethnicity in a community, with "fall" in this sense meaning the near collapse of language and community "Norwegianess" by 1950, and then the revival and survival that eventually followed.)

Getting There

We'll call our settlement "Olavstown," and locate it in a rural area in the upper Midwest (seem reasonable thus far?). The reasons for Norwegians "getting there" involve what historians call the "push-pull theory"; that is, some emigrant groups and many individuals were basically pushed, if not driven, out of their homeland (for example, Russian Jews). For Norwegians, it was primarily the "pull" of the United States with "Economic Opportunities" (read Land) being the overwhelming reason to "get there."

How did they get there? By ship, of course, but the kinds of ships used varied widely, which also meant that the time on the ocean varied widely. If they came before 1875, they might well have been on sailing ships, which took about eight, if lucky, to ten weeks to get to America. Pure misery!

Although this is a digression, it still seems useful to print the PROVISION LIST FOR TEN WEEKS AT SEA FOR ONE ADULT PERSON: 70 lbs. hard bread, 8 lbs. butter, 24 lbs. meat, 1 keg herring, 3/8 barrel potatoes, 20 lbs. rye and barley flour, 1 bushel peas, 3 lbs. coffee, 3 lbs. sugar, 2 lbs. syrup; a little salt, pepper, vinegar and onions. The ship provided three quarts of water for each person per day. Utensils needed were pots, a pail, plate, cup, spoon, knife and fork. The ship provided firewood, medicine and light. The light was much needed in steerage; that is, in the bottom of the boat, the cheapest section for travel.

147

After 1875, steam-powered ships with screw propellers reduced the sailing time to eight to ten days, if lucky. (Nowadays folks go from Minneapolis to Oslo in eight to ten hours.)

By 1900, before "getting there," there were already Norwegian "mother settlements" well established; for example, in Brooklyn, New York; Norway, Illinois; Stoughton, Wisconsin; Decorah, Iowa; Spring Grove, Minnesota; Grand Forks, North Dakota; Sioux Falls, South Dakota. New arrivals regularly spent initial time in these "springboard communities" to get semi-informed about this strange new land, and from there they'd move on to their chosen home, with some coming to the new farming region around our Olavstown. All with different stories to tell about the voyage, they would finally "get there."

Despite the Olavstown area being populated by Norwegians, they were hardly a unified group from the start. They obviously spoke Norwegian, but the great variety of dialects (were some superior?) added to long-term divisiveness. (There are 103 dialects spoken in Norway today.) Moreover, their reasons for leaving and for getting to Olavstown were different, as different as the home districts from which they came (inferior valleys back "home"?). Add to the mix the issue of city versus country along with a still-lingering "class system," and Olavstown had its internal problems from the start.

Superiority notions were real. For example, some of the earliest Lutheran pastors (from Norway, they were "upper class") complained openly in America about the lack of deference shown to them, notably by their domestic servants. However, from the maids' point of view, things were wonderfully different. Some would receive letters from Norway with the prefix before their names reading Pige, old-style-Dano-Norsk for "low-class servants." When they wrote return letters, they put a different prefix, "Miss," before their names. Good-bye class system, hello social fluidity. "Only in America" . . .

So eventually, Olavstown gained sufficient population of their own kind to live literally as "Norwegians in America." If language is at the top of the list for maintaining ethnic culture, could/would this be done? Answer: Yes, for a long while. To illustrate that point on a personal note, my grandfather, Lars Lee, emigrated at age twenty-two from Laerdal, Norway, in 1886 to a farm outside of Decorah, Iowa. He lived to be eighty-seven years old, and when he died he might have known 50 words of English. Where he lived and when he lived (and there's the explanation), 1856 to 1943, he got along fine knowing only Norse. By 1950, however, that language was foreign and essentially "gone" for the generation born in America.

> By 1950, however, that language was foreign and essentially "gone" for the generation born in America.

Setting Up The Community

What are the long-range and short-range goals of Olavstown, if any? Should there be a deliberate effort to set up a strictly Norwegian town in America? Are the new immigrants to remain Norwegians as they live their lives here? Can it be done? Should they become not Norwegian-Americans, but Norwegians living in America?

Indeed, there were some Norse settlers who believed in the goal of the latter, in effect, to set up a kind of Norwegian Quebec, almost an independent state, with the capital, of course, in Minneapolis. Then the obvious question: Should this be done by any immigrant group?

Writers Glazer and Moynihan in their book *Beyond the Melting Pot* told of non-Norwegian immigrants who had no intention of assimilating or Americanizing themselves, ever! The writers' phrase applying to these folks was "the unmeltable ethnics." The Norwegians in America, however, eventually "melted."

Although the Norse pioneers may have set up virtual enclaves like our Olavstown, it was less by doctrinaire design and more by habit of maintaining known traditions. Simply like-minded people coming together.

Thus at the turn of the twentieth century there were dozens, if not hundreds, of "lutefisk ghettoes" set up in the Midwest and on both coasts. After all, 800,000 + Norwegians came to the United States between 1825 and 1925.

With traditions in mind, let us "set up" Olavstown, but we'll just let it grow, like Topsy, and then later accept what happens. Good Scandinavian fatalistic thinking.

Where to start? Most important is the church, the focal and rallying point around which folks will get involved and later evolve. However, knowing the doctrinal disputes that arose among Norwegian-Lutheran congregations before 1900 (oh, how they fought!), we might as well plan on two churches, a "high church" and a "low church." Why? Well, consider Rollag, Minnesota, today, population 31, where two large Norwegian Lutheran churches were built almost across the road from each other. Was this necessary? In 1899, maybe. In 1999, a bigger "maybe"–only if one believes in maintaining traditions, and old grudges.

Back to the building and the buildings in Olavstown. Considering the aphorism that "we are what we eat," it is important that there be grocery stores where, of course, all the clerks talk Norwegian and where people can come to trade, trading eggs and butter for groceries, mainly on Friday nights, and there buy the necessary foods, such as pickled herring and pickled pig's feet, brown cheese and old cheese (gamelost), and, of course, torsk and lutefisk. And more.

The town needs, according to those thirsty souls so inclined for a *dram*, a saloon or two or three. And as long as there's this public sin on Main Street, there might just as well be pool tables in the back of the saloons. The saloon was a bastion of "maledom," the one place where no self-respecting woman would ever go, the unholy place where Ma would send one of the boys to fetch Pa when the trading and the "wissiting" on the streets had ended and it was time to go home.

Olavstown had enough interested readers to have their own newspaper, the *O-Town Tooter*. (Between 1865 and 1914 there were some 400 to 500 Norwegian language newspapers.) The *Tooter* can boost the town while providing the local news. More national news can come from subscribing to the Minneapolis *Tidene*, whose circulation hit 33,000 in 1910. (Today there are only two such publications left: *The Norway Times* out of Brooklyn, New York, and *The Western Viking* out of Seattle, Washington.)

> ...the unholy place where Ma would send one of the boys to fetch Pa when the trading and the "wissiting" on the streets had ended and it was time to go home.

There were a couple of cultural carryovers from the old country that needed organizing in Olavstown. First, there was an all-male chorus that citizens hoped could match the already established Luren Society in Decorah, Iowa. Second, there was the need for and the fun of folk dancing, complete with members wearing their bunads (old-world costumes), each style representing a specific area in Norway. With a couple of fiddle players, including a very special eight-stringed Hardanger violin, the shottiches and hambos and mazurkas and polkas would resound throughout the Community Hall while the dancers would pound the floor and drive out the rats holed up underneath.

Olavstown was not big enough to have its own hospital, but there's a couple of good doctors, even if one, Dr. Forde, chews snoose and for colds, prescribes *puntz* (two shots of brandy in boiling water, with sugar stirred in). And there's not enough interest to have a town theater group, despite all those great plays of Ibsen awaiting production. If folks wanted to see ethnic theater, they could go to Minneapolis, along Cedar Avenue, the section with so many Scandinavians that it was called "Snoose Boulevard." Along with theaters were Scandinavian standup comedians performing there, like Hjalmar Peterson, who used the stage name "Olle Skruthult," and who always sang the crowd's favorite request, "Nikolina."

There's already an "American problem" in Olavstown in 1900. The earliest preachers lost the good fight to teach religion in public schools, and the only way to counteract that was to start a parochial school. Not only can churches run the school properly and have religious instruction, but the teaching can be done in Norwegian. In the public school the kids may talk Norse at recess, but inside the schoolhouse it was English only.

For those families who can't or won't pay tuition to the parochial school, their kids would be taught their religion in summer schools and/or Saturday classes in the churches. Wherever the training comes, it was to lead up to the biggest day in a child's (or maybe the parents') life: confirmation into full membership in the church–the multipurpose event that moves a kid to semi-adult status overnight. On that Sunday were the best clothes worn and the best foods eaten. A most memorable day–then, in the early 1900s.

A few people wanted to start their own academy, a church-sponsored high school, but that was costly, and for most parents, eight grades of school was enough book-learning for anyone. If foolish parents wanted to waste their money, they could send their youngster off on the train to one of the 75 Norwegian-American academies operating in the Midwest. (Again, an update: Only one academy is left, Oak Grove High School in Fargo, North Dakota.)

Back to Olavstown's first building argument over a church or churches. Many inhabitants came from a "low church" background, followers of Hans Nielsen Hauge in Norway and the pastor who took up that cause in America, Erling Eielsen. Theirs was a hard, stiff-necked religion, summarized in part with declarations starting with three words: "Thou shalt not . . ." In contrast to the Haugeans were those Olavstown residents who came out of a "high church" heritage and wanted in America the same kind of politics and policies seen in the official state church of Norway, with one major difference. In America the congregations hired, and fired, the pastors. For Norwegian Lutherans gathered anywhere in America who did not want to start a big argument, whether it was in the Ladies Aids in the church basements or the men's whist groups in the fire halls, the major "no-no" topic was predestination. It had split the Norwegian Lutheran churches wide open in 1888.

> Theirs was a hard, stiff-necked religion, summarized in part with declarations starting with three words: "Thou shalt not . . ."

Along with the usual, if not expected, church disputes, there were all kinds of national issues that new Olavstown folks had to deal with—emotional and moral things, like temperance. Should the townspeople form their own Temperance Society? And does temperance mean total abstinence from alcohol or only moderation in consumption? How about those American political parties and some of the "-isms" connected to them? Should they be like the Finns and tend toward Socialism and join unions, even like the radical Industrial Workers of the World? The Wobblies? That union denounced capitalism as evil. How do we vote and what do we join or not join? The Masons? The Elks Lodge? It's safest to join the Sons of Norway and take our insurance from that company started by a few Norsk immigrants in Minneapolis, the Lutheran Brotherhood.

By 1910 Olavstown was "set up" and "on its way"– to where, nobody knew. Just let it happen. Meanwhile, don't openly discriminate against the few non-Norwegians in town. Just ignore them, the poor things.

In summary, communities like Olavstown were typical and representative ethnic towns in the ways they were "set up." The citizens established a culture that they knew and liked, and yet from the very beginning they were subject to melting pot pressures, the need to assimilate, to Americanize. Time, the great healer, would also become the great stealer, stealing away the old ways by 1950. Those old ways would unravel in two generations.

The Community Matures

About a dozen years after Olavstown began, powerful forces for change fell on the community. The major forces began outside the United States, in Europe, in the summer of 1914 when what was labeled The Great War started in August, and one by one countries tumbled into the cauldron of war. At the start it seemed to Americans like "none of our business," with even President Wilson calling on citizens to be neutral. But they were not. Too many Americans, old and new, had families directly involved "over there" not to take sides. Officially, Norway was neutral, but little by little the large Norwegian merchant fleet was being sunk by mines and German *unterwasser* boats (submarines). By war's end, Norway lost half its fleet. The Norwegian-American press had already taken sides–and opposite sides–before the sinkings started.

War aside, generational conflicts had already set in at Olavstown. The children born and coming of age in America were far less interested in maintaining old-world ways. Some young folks viewed their parents as anachronisms, out of touch with the American real world. Some became embarrassed by their elders' manners and speech, and the translating for them that became more and more necessary. Uff da. After all, the young folks were coming-of-age Americans whose bilingualism was at first taken for granted, but the young adults also viewed their ethnic-dominated life around them as out of step with mainstream society. A culture clash.

Historian Marcus Hansen in *The Atlantic Migration* observed that although all generations at all times have their differences, the generation for which the generation-gap was most difficult were the children of the immigrants. The kids had to live, adapt and survive in two different worlds, the one of their parents and the one of America around them.

The Great War, eventually renamed World War I, would do more than any other event in the twentieth century to set back ethnicity. Old-world ways, notably foreign languages, were not only frowned upon, they were viewed as un-American, if not traitorous, once the United States entered the War in 1917.

"Patriots" in 1918 cheered the order of Iowa's Governor Harding, who decreed that from henceforth the only language that could be spoken in that state was "American!" Wartime hysteria had taken over. Prescribed loyalties were not only encouraged, they were forced on United States citizens.

Taking the brunt of wartime attacks at home were, of course, German-Americans, leading to what would be the low point of mistreatment for any immigrant group, all in the name of patriotism. Theirs is a separate, sad story. It led to a heritage deferred, if not devastated.

Scandinavian-Americans were caught on the very fringe of the anti-German hysteria because they were, after all, Lutherans, followers of the doctrines of Martin Luther, a German. Suddenly it became necessary for Scandinavian Lutherans in America to work extra hard to demonstrate their loyalty, and among the several open acts of patriotism was to display the American flag in their churches. A flag is an emotional symbol that cuts to the heart of one's loyalties, but does a secular symbol belong in church?

When the young men in military service returned to their hometowns after the war ended in November of 1918, they were as changed as the world had been changed by the carnage in Europe. It had allegedly been "the war to end all wars," but it did not turn out that way, and growing cynicism rolled gradually across the nation. In a different way; "it's none of our business" would be applied to American views toward Europe in the 1920s. So the United States does not join the League of Nations. We blame our problems on "foreigners" and pass new immigration laws (the Johnson Act, 1924) to stop letting large numbers in, create a quota system, and rig it to keep out most southern and eastern Europeans and all Asians. The end of an age. As to those "foreigners" already here, discourage any more old-world "maintenance" and make President Wilson's negative views well known on what he sarcastically called "hyphenated Americans."

In places like Olavstown, the discouragement of old-world ways was more the result of time taking its toll. By 1930 many of the original settlers had passed on; only for them were funeral services conducted in Norwegian. English had slipped into church worship once a month when the war was on. Then came English services twice a month, and soon more and more English so that by 1940 Norwegian church services were available only for special holidays like Christmas and Easter.

Bold young adults were marrying both out of the Norwegian Evangelical Lutheran Church and out of their ethnic heritage. These initial acts took great bravery for couples and produced anxieties and anguish for the parents and families of both the bride and the groom. After all, Roman Catholic parents were just as "disgraced" as the Lutherans by this–this near treachery of their children. Some became "ex-children" who were renounced and dismissed by the parents and told never to come home again.

Around town things had changed. "Foreigners" from other towns had moved in and were making plans to start a Methodist church. Even a few families with French background were making noises about the town celebrating Bastille Day, whatever that was. And a family named Petrowski bought the furniture store!

> By 1930 many of the original settlers had passed on; only for them were funeral services conducted in Norwegian.

Except for one mossback columnist, the *Tooter* newspaper was all in English by 1930, with a young editor pushing for the construction of a public high school. He said they were the wave of the future and that any town that did not have a high school by 1930 would mean the end of the town because parents would follow, and shop, wherever their children went to school. Simple: no public schools, no towns. They'll dry up, and at best turn into bedroom communities for bigger towns.

The decade of the '30s, the Depression years, made even more severe dents, if not smashes, into that now aging idea of maintaining ethnic heritage. After all, who can afford to pay their dues to the Sons of Norway Lodge? Same with the costs of keeping the Folk Dance Society going. Same with buying subscriptions to Norsk language newspapers and magazines. Let 'em all go. Economic survival is what's important. Expensive lutefisk can only be served once a year, at Christmastime. For the rest of the year, it's basic grøt (poor oatmeal) to eat, and regularly left-over leftovers. Could things ever get worse?

Maybe not worse, certainly not economically, but total-ly different by the 1940s, and so disruptive to all American society when World War II began in 1941. First things first. That meant to do whatever needed to be done to win the war. Even small communities like Olavstown were affected. Indeed, World War II is the single most impor-tant event in the century to change the entire world! Nothing would ever be the same again for any nation or any community within that nation. Ethnic heritage, what little was left, was an insignificant side interest; at war's end it was still off to the side. Another generation had gone off to war and returned, if lucky, more as citizens of the world than Norwegian-Americans. And another era had ended. By 1950 notions like maintaining or celebrat-ing or promoting heritage were at best dormant. Not dead, just comatose. Would/could/should they ever be res-urrected? Likely not. Off to the ash heaps of history. A vic-tory for the melting pot.

Decline and Survival

In this final section, the fictional Olavstown of 1950 will be replaced by a real Norwegian-American town, appropriately named Scandinavia, located in central Wisconsin (and my hometown). This prototype communi-ty represented totally the four-stage pattern of changes, but unlike Olavstown, it went further back, starting in the 1850s, and became one of those "mother settlements" to which fresh immigrants came first for orientation before leaving soon for other "lutefisk ghettoes." The first church in Scandinavia was also a "mother church," in that four other regional churches spun off from the mother.

Scandinavia also had an academy (started in 1893) and it later added a two-year college course (1920), which led to its renaming, Central Wisconsin College (CWC). In the school pattern that followed, CWC went under in the Depression and the school became a public four-year high school in 1933. (It needs to be added that in Scandinavia, my father was the president of CWC and later the supervising principal of the high school.)

Anyway, as to this section, in 1950, organized religion in town was back to the "singular," back to one church and one congregation. There had been a split long before (in 1890), which led to two churches, but after the demise of one generation, the two churches became one again in 1917. To reflect the new times, the national church synod in 1946 dropped the name Norwegian from its official title and it became simply the Evangelical Lutheran Church.

One town ethnic event–and one of the very few remaining by 1950–still continued, the annual fall Lutefisk Supper, but by then meatballs had been added to the menu. To the older adults, the supper was important and a tradition to maintain. To the young adults, it was of questionable importance and probably not worth continuing. Within the next ten years, the suppers were canceled–not enough younger workers to keep it going.

The changes in businesses downtown reflected also the "maturing process." A Polish–and Catholic–family took over the hardware store. A German family–and Methodists–bought the drugstore. The only Jewish family in town left, following a fire that completely destroyed their big general store. It was their third store fire (don't think the tongues didn't wag for years after that one). The welding shop reopened, its owner having returned from Alaska where he had worked on the Alaskan highway during the war. One grocery store had been purchased by a returning G.I., and he was another non-Norwegian and non-Lutheran.

Despite the above changes, the town still remained primarily Norwegian. To illustrate how theoretically Norwegian we were, consider the last names of the high school basketball team and the cheerleaders in 1949, the year this author graduated. The starting five: Moe, Mork, Erickson, Lee and Taylor (the latter two spellings had been Americanized). The remaining squad members: Anderson, Gjertson, Nelson, Gudmandsen and Wasrud. Cheerleaders: Jenson, Olson, Erickson, Jorgesen and Mork. The coach was named Christensen.

With only a few exceptions, all of the above student names had one or more grandparents who were immigrants, and parents who could and did talk Norwegian at home, using Norsk primarily when they did not want their children to understand what they were talking about. Now to the point about what happened to "Norwegianess." None of the above-named players or cheerleaders could either understand or read or speak Norwegian, other than a couple basic lines and phrases, along with a few swear words. Just as significant in this "passage"–nobody old or young cared about the near total loss of the language.

Downtown on the streets and in the stores and taverns, one could still hear Norwegian spoken in 1950, but only by older folks. There were no efforts made by adults to promote language training, and likely had there been such an effort, the young people would have resisted it, mainly out of apathy. We were good at that.

Celebrations of heritage were gone. *Sytende Mai*, May 17, Norway's Constitution Day, the biggest day for celebrations there, was totally ignored by their direct ancestors living in our America. By 1950 in our town, it was as important as Bastille Day, whatever that was.

One tavern was called "Little Norway," but the title would be more historic than relevant to postwar United States. Except for a table of Norse-speaking oldsters back in the corner playing whist, there were left just two standard sentences used when two people met:

The first one said, *"Aasen gar det?"* ("How's it going?")

The second replied, *"Bare bra, takk."* ("Pretty good, thanks.")

And then both went to English.

All of the above is perhaps sufficient to illustrate the decline of culture and maintenance in this one town, but similar towns and city neighborhoods went the same way. Even some Norwegian-American church colleges not only did not uphold their heritage, but also contributed to the general decline. For example, Luther College, Decorah, Iowa, by 1950 dropped its requirement for graduation that all students must take at least one full year of either Norwegian or "Norwegian Culture." Ethnic downtime there and almost everywhere else. 'Twas a long waning period for "Norwegianess" in the 1950s and 1960s. Worse, the decline suggested the coming complete demise of the heritage. But who cares?

> **Downtown on the streets and in the stores and taverns, one could still hear Norwegian spoken in 1950, but only by older folks.**

Somebody cared. Indeed, many cared because slowly, very slowly, in incremental small steps taken by individuals and groups in many states, an ethnic Lazarus (alas, not a Norwegian) made a revival. By 1975, the restoration was well on its way.

In fairness, of course, it was never totally dead. (Is that like being half pregnant?) Organizations such as the sons of Norway and the Norsemen's Federation had hung in there and kept going, often on shoestring budgets. However, around 1970, the times became right for new interest and growth. Concerted efforts led to increased memberships and more lodges. An awakening was happening, although nobody knows exactly why.

Again, as to never "dead," there were those stalwart half dozen major universities who had maintained their Scandinavian studies programs. The University of North Dakota–and talk about the power of its founders–never failed in any year to carry out its mandate that Norwegian shall always be taught at that school! The academics had had their insular, if not isolated, groups; for example, the Society for the Advancement of Scandinavian Studies, which went back to 1928. By the 1970s, however, members stopped talking only to each other and opened things up, sponsoring public meetings and conferences at Scandinavian church colleges again, eager and willing to be part of this "Great Ethnic Awakening."

St. Olaf College in Northfield, Minnesota, would be the headquarters for what too many Norwegian-Americans was the best-kept secret of their harboring "the best ethnic-history-society in the country, the Norwegian-American Historical Association (NAHA)." (That designation was bestowed on NAHA by a non-Norwegian director of the Minnesota Historical Society, Russell Fridley.)

Come to the Festivals

However, what really caught the attention of not just Scandinavians but all citizens in the last quarter of the twentieth century have been the many and large Scandinavian festivals, most held annually–and each lasting longer, getting better, attracting bigger crowds every year. For example, Minot, North Dakota, civic leaders believed in 1972 that a public event they would call HØST-FEST ("Fall Festival"/"Harvest Festival") would be an appropriate action to honor the many Scandinavians who in large numbers helped settle the Dakotas. HØSTFEST began as a small two-day celebration that attracted a couple hundred people, but it was later judged successful enough to do it again the following year, and the following, and by the 1990s HØSTFEST turned into a five-day festival, bringing in some 60,000 folks each fall from dozens of states and Canada. The interest and the numbers have made it nearly impossible for attendees to find a motel within 100 miles of Minot during HØSTFEST. Although billed as "all-Scandinavian," big-name entertainers were brought in to build the huge crowds, names like Bill Cosbyson, Jay Leno-son, Barbara Mandrells-dotter, The Stattlerson Brothers, et al.

If HØSTFEST advertises as the biggest indoor festival (all doings held in the state fair buildings), the biggest outdoor and indoor celebration war is NORDIC FEST in Decorah, Iowa, (starting in 1966) held the third weekend in July, complete with a Sunday morning Main Street parade. This small city of 10,000 people quadruples in size for NORDIC FEST. Although an effort was made to honor equally all-Scandinavian immigrants, things Norwegian seemed to outnumber the others.

More communities have started their own festivals, such as Eau Claire and Stoughton, Wisconsin, and Willmar and Fargo-Moorhead, Minnesota, to name only a few, but Decorah has a year-round advantage in interest because there is located Vesterheim ('Western Home"), the largest Norwegian-American museum in the United States. Its vast numbers and displays of artifacts require both inside and outside room, the latter on expanding land behind the major museum building where there have been moved a variety of buildings/structures to illustrate "old Norway in new Amerika."

The newer promotions, like the festivals, would, of course, build on older, established, honored entities, whether major institutions like Swedish hospitals or smaller places like Finnish-sponsored nursing homes. Ethnic names became important once again. (Even new babies were given "old world" names.)

New heritage centers, like the well-established Vesterheim and the American Swedish Institute, were also built by the Finns in Hancock, Michigan, and by the Danes in Elkhorn, Iowa, the latter location to the dismay of many Danish-Americans living around Solvang, California. Icelanders, always tiny in numbers, can still find Icelandic culture continued in towns such as Minneota, Minnesota, and Pembina, North Dakota. (There were many more Icelandic immigrants to Canada than to the United States. They are a regular part of Winnipeg's annual festival called FOLKLORAMA.)

As in most human relationships, so, too, in ethnic heritage continuation, it is the little things that count. Yet, depending on the persons or families, they're not little at all. They can be big in importance. Things like Scandinavian furniture, jewelry, clothes, weaving, crocheting, wood carving, scroll carving, sewing, embroidery, decorations and more. If all of the above are desired but cannot be easily accomplished, all are available for purchase at the many Scandinavian gift stores.

Just as available are Scandinavian magazines and books and music. The latter can range from the high art of Edvard Grieg or Johan Svendsen to the low art (but authentic and fun) folk music of groups like LeRoy Larson and his Scandinavian Ensemble, or singer/ comedian Stan Boreson.

Inadvertently, as to any preplanning by leaders, both Norwegians and Lutherans have become nationally "famous," thanks to the popular Saturday radio show called "A Prairie Home Companion." However, the fact that radio host Garrison Keillor's fun with his ethnic groups teeters on the fine line between gentle satire and ridicule bothers/disgusts many sensitive listeners. Whenever Keillor mentions Lake Wobegon's "Statue of the Unknown Norwegian," it always gets a laugh, but some listeners are not amused. Ah, the price of fame. (?)

It can be said now that Scandinavian heritage in America has not only survived, it has thrived by the year 2000. Accepting that premise requires one to discount the fact that in the survival and revival, the original languages have been essentially lost. Now the good news. There's a revival in that area, too, thanks to the growth of "language camps." Illustrative is the work of Concordia College, Moorhead, Minnesota, which back in 1963 started one camp on a northern lake near Bemidji and called it *Skogfjorden* ("Lake of the Woods"). To this single camp have come thousands of young people–little kids and big kids–and adults, too. Once the students arrive, it's "total immersion" in things Norwegian the entire time they're there. In the dining hall kids learn quickly to say the words smør and brød or nobody will pass them the bread and butter.

> It can be said now that Scandinavian heritage in America has not only survived, it has thrived by the year 2000.

The first Norwegian camp was so successful that more and bigger camps have been built on the same acreage, each a separate "village" set off by all the buildings having the architectural designs of the country it represents. Visitors can thus "travel from country to country," all within 680 acres. For the many thoughtful Americans who worried that "foreign languages"–and they're not so foreign anymore–would be lost forever, these language camps throughout the country have proven to be saviors. 'Tis a good thing, and only one of many examples to indicate clearly that . . .

THE SCANDINAVIAN HERITAGE IS ALIVE AND WELL. ITS SURVIVAL IS ENSURED, GOING INTO THE TWENTY-FIRST CENTURY.

With that in mind, let us relax and enjoy it. Say, did you hear the story about Lars Trulson and Truls Larson? No? Well, then, it goes like this . . .

THE END

And, as the Norwegians might say, "Till Slutt." ("Finally.") There are still the romantics among us to whom the past means almost as much as the future, and who take pleasure in tracing our heritage back through the generations and sometimes through the centuries. You, the reader, must be one of them, for otherwise you would not have read this book.

About the Author—

(who says "History can be fun." Really!):

His nine books contain both serious and comic material, in effect relating what everyday life is like. Art Lee at this writing (2000) is a Professor Emeritus of History at Bemidji State University, Minnesota, where he taught for 35 years.

Lee's interest in things Scandinavian came understandably and naturally, having been born, raised and schooled in a Norwegian-American town named Scandinavia, in central Wisconsin; also three of his four grandparents were emigrants from Norway.

(In a sort of reverse migration, one of his daughters married a Norwegian and she and her family live in Grimstad, Norway.)

Lee's formal education came at three colleges where there were strong Scandinavian programs: Luther College, Decorah, Iowa; and the Universities of Wisconsin and North Dakota.

Three of his books are strictly about the life and times in Scandinavian-America —The Lutefisk Ghetto, Leftover Lutefisk, and Leftover Lefse. His straight history books include University in the Pines: A History of Bemidji State University, 1919-1994. He also has an article in a recent publication of the Norwegian American Historical Association.

Special honors to Dr. Lee came with his twice being voted "Outstanding Teacher of the Year" at Bemidji State, and soon after his retirement in 1995, the University named a large lecture-hall after him.

Lee remains active as a speaker, and while out on the hustings, where he meets many folks with stories to tell him, he remains on the watch for that rarest of "birds" so hard to find— a good Scandinavian joke that he has never heard before.

Art Lee and his wife Judy have three children and four grandchildren; they make their summer home in Bemidji and winter in Arizona.

All decked out in their scandinavian Sunday best...

Author Art Lee (center) with Lodge officers of the Tucson Norse Federation. On the left is Gretchen Carew, who summers in Minnesota; on the right is Anna-Marie Nelson, a resident of Tucson but still a Norwegian citizen.